SUPER SMALLS

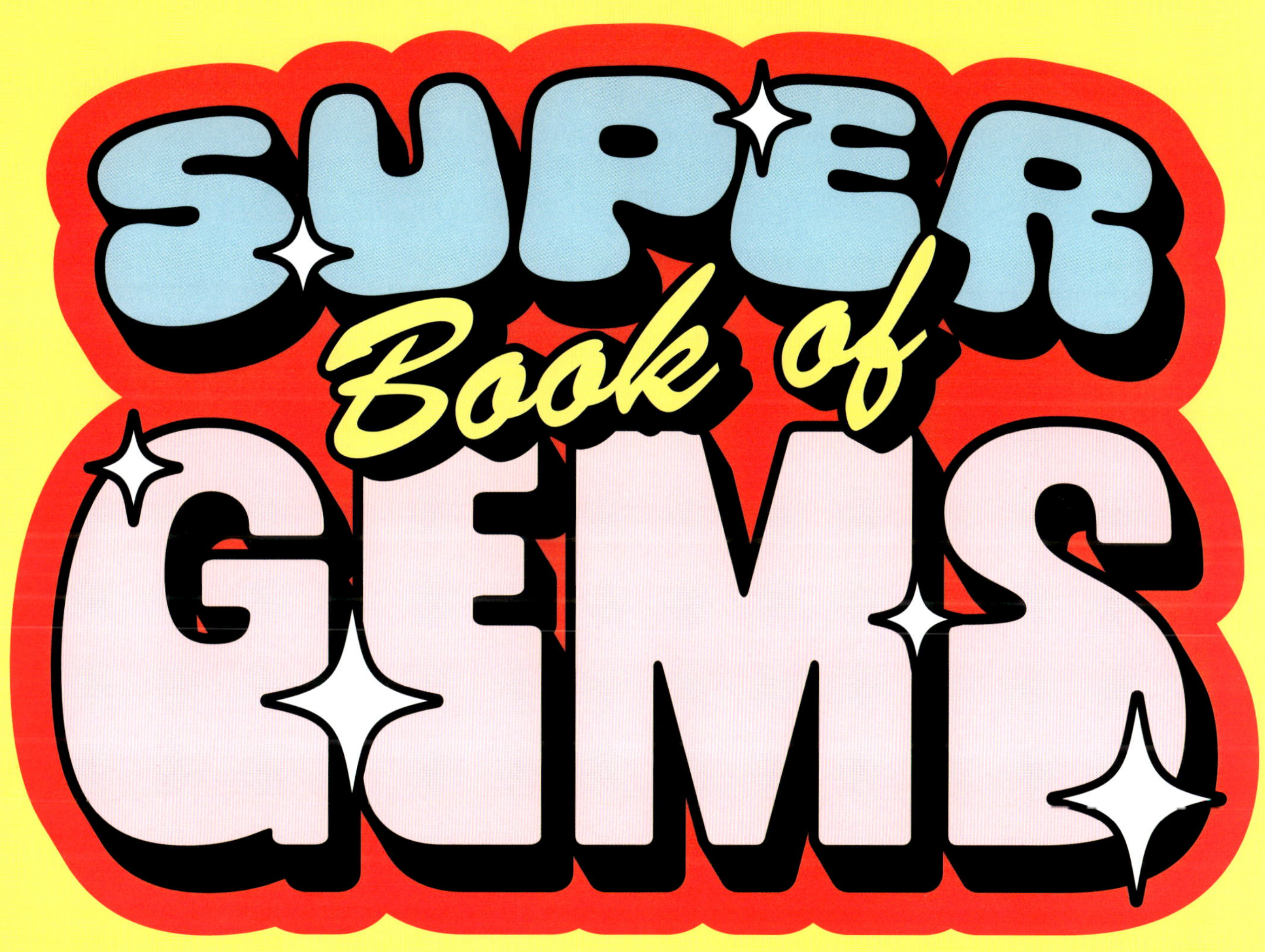

SUPER
SMALLS

Maria Dueñas Jacobs &
Bianca Gottesman

UNION
SQUARE
& CO.
NEW YORK

**To our little gems, Luna, Isa, Silvi, Gabi, and Rafa: You gave this book its sparkle. We love you endlessly.**

## Gemstone Primer



## Birthstones

Science & Splendor

# Foreword

For as long as I have been writing about jewelry, there have been certain universal jewelry truths I have tried to establish. Jewelry has meaning—we choose it to mark life's biggest decisions and moments of happiness. Jewelry is history—kings and queens are made such by golden crowns and diadems, and the twists and turns of each era imprint themselves visibly and undeniably on jewelry design (see: Egyptian Revival bracelets, Art Nouveau necklaces, Retro period cuffs, Edwardian tassels). And maybe most importantly? Jewelry is fun. Watch what happens when you are wearing a pair of earrings and you pick up a baby. They go straight for them. Shiny beautiful things appeal to all ages.

But it's more than that. Or it can be. Share the fantastical tales behind stones' many myths and legends, speak of the magical properties of rubies and emeralds and aquamarines and amethyst, and you will have a jewelry lover for life. Begin immediately.

The Dueñas sisters, Maria Dueñas Jacobs and Bianca Gottesman, make it easy. Super Smalls, the company they founded in 2019, encourages people of all ages to actually play with jewelry. That intimidation you feel when you walk into a store of vitrines packed with diamonds? Super Smalls, with its gem-studded headbands, deliberately enormous cocktail rings, bead kits, and vanity kits with stones of all shapes and shades and sizes, encourages you not to be afraid. The same way you might watch a child place ten Super Smalls rings on

her hands is how all jewelry should be approached: with joy. Relish in the sparkle, delight in the details. Even if you never buy a single piece—although I encourage you to, of course—jewelry can be enjoyed and appreciated.

This book takes that sense of true engagement with jewelry deeper. It is meant to be shared—not locked in a vault or kept high on a bookshelf, out of reach. It takes the delight that Super Smalls brings to jewelry and adds deeper meaning—the great houses are here, and all those great stories about where stones come from and what they mean—while never sacrificing the childlike wonder we all feel when we first spot a ring we love in a store window. What this book, and these sisters, do is push you to not only stare at it through the glass but to walk in and ask about it, find out what the center stone is, where it was discovered, and what powers it holds—and, yes, to ask them to take that ring out so you can try it on. The same way you might have delighted in playing with your mother's charm bracelet as a child, or a Super Smalls necklace during a kid's dress-up party.

Super Smalls has unlocked the happiness potential in all jewels, for all ages. This book continues the mission.

**STELLENE VOLANDES**
Editor in Chief, *Town & Country*
Editorial Director, *Elle Decor*
Jewelry Lover and Author

# Welcome to the Super-Sparkly World of Gems

In these pages, we'll dive deep into the magic, mysticism, and science surrounding some of our favorite stones, uncovering their meanings and extraordinary features.

Perhaps you've heard the word *birthstone* before—maybe you even know yours already. Maybe you already wear a piece of jewelry connected to when you were born, which—as you're about to find out—is a super-popular custom across the globe.

If you're new to the world of birthstones: Welcome. You're going to love it here!

The word *birthstone* is used to describe a number of rare and special gems that are cosmically linked to the time of year you were born. Starting way back in time—we're talking whole centuries ago!—certain naturally occurring rocks and minerals caught the attention of people across cultures and continents. These stones were inexplicably beautiful—with the power to elicit feelings of awe and wonder. Those feelings were MAGICAL, and our awestruck, jewel-loving ancestors decided that carrying and wearing these rare gemstones held meaning and might offer them protection from harm or bring them good luck.

In Western tradition, birthstones are tied to the month you were born. In Eastern tradition, birthstones are tied to your astrological sign and a celestial body (think: the moon, stars, planets, comets, etc!). As Western and Eastern traditions have intermingled, the mystical reputations of gemstones have grown, as has the belief that wearing a birthstone can enhance your natural attributes and strengths because who doesn't love a little magic or need an extra boost?

No two cultures have the exact same set of birthstones, and the modern birthstone list continues to grow! Gemologists and jewelers have tweaked the list multiple times in the past century, adding newly popular stones and making space for dazzling color variations.

Some months have been tied to their original, one-and-only birthstone since people started keeping track of these things, but other months have been linked to multiple stones over time.

Have a birthday in June, October, or December? Lucky you—these months have a variety of shimmering birthstones to choose from.

January, February, March, April, May, July, August, September, and November birthdays have just one birthstone each—these months are paired with heavy-hitter gems like diamonds, rubies, and sapphires!

A sparkling jewel cosmically linked to the month you were born is a super-cool place to start your gem adventure, but these brilliant treasures have so many intriguing facets to explore. Ready for more gemstone magic? Turn the page and let's go!

# What is a Gem?

A gem is a precious or semiprecious stone that is cherished for its beauty—both physical and symbolic. Historically, three main physical attributes have been used to qualify, identify, and describe gems.

## BEAUTY

This is all about a gem's visual appeal. It's not just about being pretty, though! Gems interact with light in fascinating ways, creating an array of colors, lusters, and that captivating sparkle we all love. Gemologists use the famous "4Cs" (cut, clarity, color, and carat weight) to assess a gem's beauty scientifically. But remember, beauty can be subjective—we can all be dazzled in different ways and by different things!

## DURABILITY

This factor tells us how well a gem can withstand the test of time. Some gems, like diamonds, are incredibly tough and can remain unchanged for millions of years. Others, like pearls, require more delicate care. A gem's durability doesn't always affect its value, though—some of the most prized gems are also quite delicate.

## RARITY

All natural gems are relatively rare, but some are true geological marvels. Gems form deep within our Earth under specific conditions, and the processes that bring them to the surface (like volcanoes and tectonic shifts) often break them into tiny pieces. Large, flawless gems are exceptionally uncommon, which contributes to their value and allure.

Beyond these physical characteristics, gems are adored the world over for the way they make people feel. Many gemstones are hundreds of millions—sometimes billions!—of years old. Gems connect their wearers with some of the rarest elements within our planet. They offer insight into our planet's composition, whether deep down beneath the surface where diamonds are formed (hundreds of miles down in Earth's mantle), or closer to the surface, like amber, which is formed by tree resin and contains the story of the plants and animals around it. Gemstones are not only a window into the scientific world around us; many people believe they offer a connection to magic and mystical forces that we cannot see or touch but that we can feel.

# What's your birthstone?!

July
Ruby

April
DIAMOND

May
Emerald

June
Pearl &
MOONSTONE

October
OPAL & PINK
TOURMALINE

November
Citrine

December
Turquoise
& Tanzanite

# January
# Garnet

# January Garnet

**Attention,** all January-born jewels! Your birthstone is the garnet, a gemstone as red as a ripe pomegranate. Throughout history, garnets were believed to have special powers to protect their wearers from harm or illness and to light up the night with their fiery glow. That's not all: Garnets were also thought to strengthen friendships and bring good luck (the jewel form of a four-leaf clover!). The garnet is the perfect gem to start the year filled with health and good fortune.

Marlo Laz garnet, diamond, and gold "Bonheur" necklace

Ancient intaglio garnet ring, late 1st century BCE

## Lol!

**Why did the unpolished garnet go to the doctor?**

It was feeling a little rough.

Asprey garnet daisy necklace

**The name *garnet* comes from the Latin word *granatus*, which means "containing many seeds" and refers to the gemstone's resemblance to a pomegranate seed!**

## Color Spectrum

**Garnets come in red, green, yellow, and purple—practically every color except blue! They can be opaque or translucent, with a glass-like finish.**

Emily P. Wheeler yellow gold, garnet, rubellite, and sapphire cuff

## Fun Fact!

**In medieval Europe, garnets were thought to prevent nightmares. Sweet dreams!**

Bulgari garnet and diamond earrings

Tiffany & Co. gold, garnet, and diamond ring

Glenn Spiro garnet bracelet

## Symbolism & Meaning

**Protection, strength, and regeneration**

**Believed to help balance energy, inspire love, and promote good health**

Pomellato garnet cabochon ring

## Specs

| CHEMICAL COMPOSITION | HARDNESS |
|---|---|
| Silicate minerals | 6.5–7.5 on the Mohs' scale |

Each day is a
GEM,

different in kind, size and color, and yours to

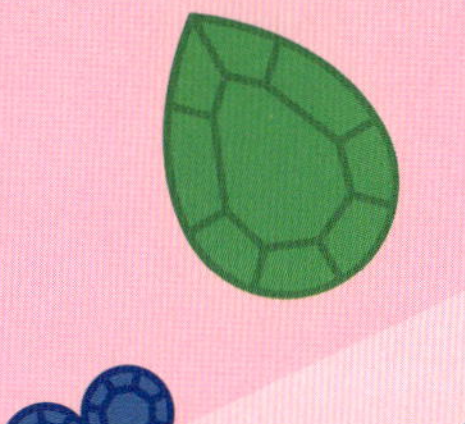

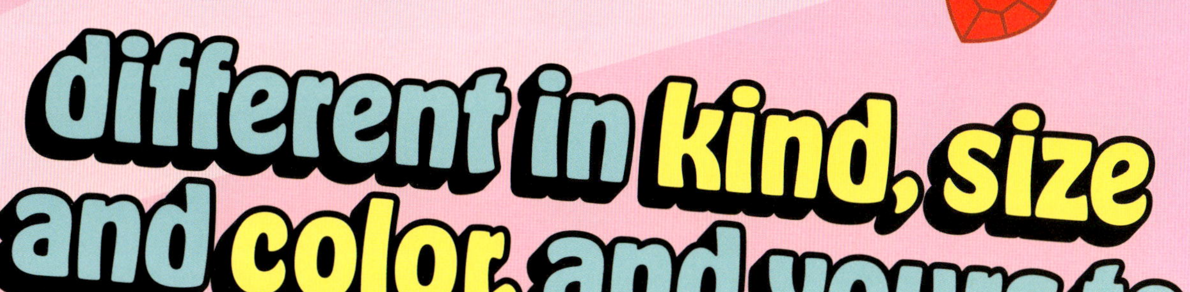

# POLISH!

— CAROLANNE REYNOLDS

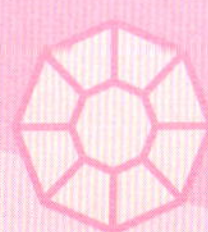

# February
# AMETHYST

# February
# AMETHYST

February visionaries! Your birthstone is the powerful amethyst, a stone with a magical reputation for bringing peace, wisdom, and clarity, like a magic spell that helps you stay calm and focused—in gem form! Amethysts are believed to impart superpowers like intuition and spiritual awareness. Even the Renaissance mastermind Leonardo da Vinci believed these purple gems could enhance intelligence and banish negative thoughts—a fifteenth-century take on boosting your brainpower and lifting your spirits!

## Haha!

**Why did the amethyst start a band?**

Because it really rocked!

Tiffany & Co. amethyst and diamond ring

## Fun Fact!

**Amethyst is often called bishop's stone because of how frequently it was featured in the rings of Catholic bishops.**

*Van Cleef & Arpels amethyst and diamond bracelet*

**An amethyst's color can fade over time due to exposure to sunlight, so be sure to store these stones in a safe place!**

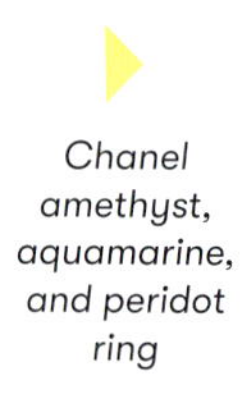

*Chanel amethyst, aquamarine, and peridot ring*

*Cartier amethyst, turquoise, and diamond turtle brooch*

Cartier amethyst, turquoise, and diamond "Les Delices de Goa" necklace

## Symbolism & Meaning

**Peace, courage, and stability**

**Believed to help with emotional balance, improve intuition, and promote clarity**

House of Fabergé pendant by Albert Holmstrom

Bulgari amethyst, colored sapphire, and diamond pendant earrings

Buccellati amethyst and yellow, pink, and white gold cuff

## Specs

| CHEMICAL COMPOSITION | HARDNESS |
| --- | --- |
| Silicon dioxide with trace amounts of iron | 7 on the Mohs' scale |

# Cut to Perfection: A Guide to Shapes & Cuts

A gemstone's cut refers to how it interacts with light. The words jewelers and gemologists use to describe how the light interacts are brightness, fire, and scintillation.

Each cut possesses its own unique, sparkling magic. In these pages, we'll explore how gems are transformed into glittering shapes meant to enhance each stone's best qualities—with symbolism and sparkle for every taste!

## Resplendent Round

This classic, and ultra-popular, gem cut shines like the brightest star. It has a perfectly symmetrical shape designed to make light dance and twinkle. This is a stone of timeless elegance—and is far and away the most in-demand cut for all diamonds!

## MARVELOUS MARQUISE

Shaped like a sleek boat or elongated eye, the marquise cut has pointed ends and an unconventional silhouette, adding a touch of sophistication to any gem—and allowing it to stand out in the jewelry seas. Rumor has it that the shape was designed at the request of the eighteenth-century French king Louis XV, who wanted a gem to resemble a woman's lips!

## Polished Princess

One of the most popular square cuts is the princess shape, featuring a sleek square appearance with a pyramidal structure that skillfully conceals imperfections and dazzles with bold sparkle and modern glamour.

## Playful Pear

A droplet of delight! The pear cut debuted in 1475, around the same year the skeif, or diamond-polishing wheel, was invented. Half round, half marquise, this playful shape is perfect for those who want a bit of whimsy in their gem collection.

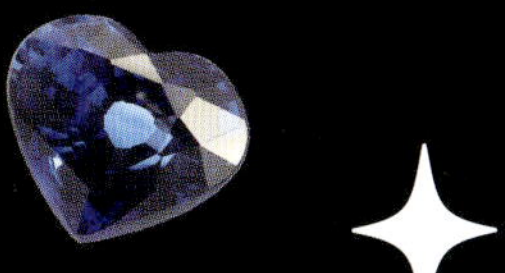

## Heartfelt Heart

A gem cut that's pure romance, crafted to symbolize love and affection, making it the perfect choice for those who wear their heart on their sleeves (or fingers)!

## RADIANT RECTANGLE/ ELEVATED EMERALD

Commanding lines, a stretched shape, and linear facets create rare and dramatic flashes of light. The shape's clean edges and modern symmetry are perfect for those who prize understated luxury.

## OUTSTANDING OVAL

With elegant curves and a timeless appeal, this shape is perfect for those who appreciate a classic look with a touch of modern flair. The elongated shapes are also known to trick the eye and make a stone appear larger!

## Plush Pillow/ Cushion

An antique cut that is fashionable and romantic—the cushion cut's soft lines and larger facets mean this shape is full of fire. This cut is most sparkly in candlelight!

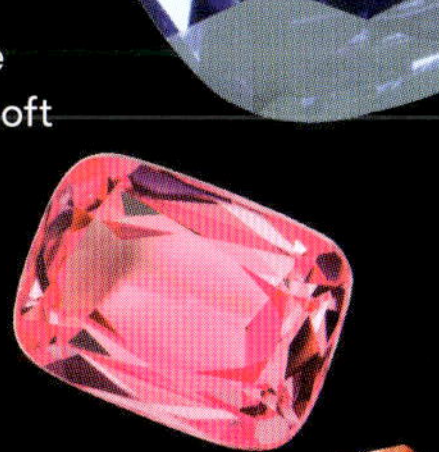

## THRILLING TRILLIANT

With its tight angles and brilliant facets, this shape creates a play of light that's nothing short of spectacular. Bursting onto the scene in the 1960s, this fiery gem knows how to party.

## Alluring Asscher

Known for its vintage elegance, this cut is a square shape with cropped corners and step-cut facets that create a "hall of mirrors" for maximum dazzle. Famous in the art deco era, this cut remains a sparkly favorite even today!

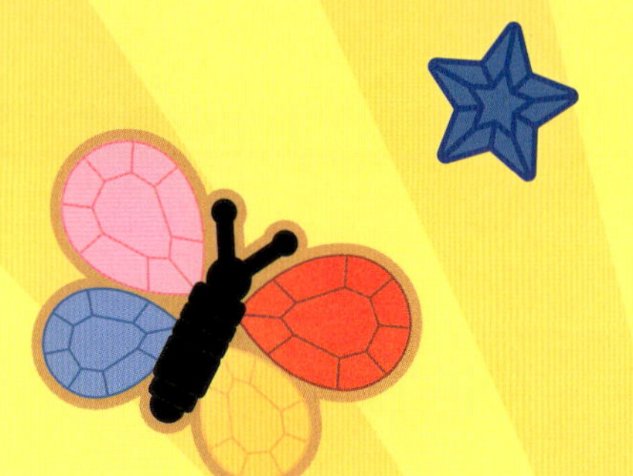

# There is no BETTER

DESIGNER

than nature.

— ALEXANDER MCQUEEN

# March
# AQUAMARINE

# March

# AQUAMARINE

**March** mermaids! Ready for a splash of magic? March's birthstone is the aquamarine, a gemstone that packs a powerful punch of courage, luck, and truth. It's said to keep wearers calm and thoughtful, like ocean waves. Aquamarine may bestow the power to speak your mind, stay cool under pressure, and find inspiration. Plus, this stone's impressive durability ensures that its enchanting qualities endure, making its "superpowers" truly long-lasting.

**LOL!**

**Why did the aquamarine go to school?**

To learn its A, B, seas!

*Oscar Heyman aquamarine, platinum, and diamond ring*

## Fun Fact!

**Long ago, sailors used aquamarine as a talisman to protect their ships on dangerous voyages.**

*Verdura aquamarine, gold, platinum, and diamond brooch*

## COLOR SPECTRUM

**Aquamarine gets its name from the Latin words *aqua* (water) and *marina* (of the sea), which describe its beautiful blue-green color.**

*Buccellati aquamarine, diamond, and yellow and white gold ring*

*Mikimoto aquamarine ring*

*Bulgari aquamarine and pink tourmaline necklace*

*Van Cleef & Arpels aquamarine and diamond "Hawaii" demi-parure earrings and brooch*

*Van Cleef & Arpels aquamarine, platinum, and diamond necklace*

## Symbolism & Meaning

**Calmness, honesty, and loyalty**

**Believed to bring good luck, protect against evil, and promote strong communication skills**

## Specs

| CHEMICAL COMPOSITION | HARDNESS |
|---|---|
| Beryl with traces of iron | 7.5–8 on the Mohs' scale |

# Made with Magic: A Selection of Stones and their Superpowers

No ordinary gems here! These sparkling stones contain multitudes. Read on to learn more about the awe-inspiring—and downright magical!—properties these gemstones are said to possess. This roster of jewels is full of supernatural powers, offering their wearers protection, luck, and all kinds of good vibes.

## RESILIENT ONYX

### THE DARK DEFENDER

A protector against negative energies, this stone helps ward off troubling thoughts and distractions. Especially useful on new adventures and nerve-racking challenges—be it a sports competition or a sleepover.

## Inspiring Opal

### THE COLORFUL THINKER

As one of the most vibrant stones, opal encourages emotional expression and creativity. It reflects the unique energy of each of us, symbolizing hope and spontaneity. Keep this on hand for special occasions or when in need of inspiration.

## INSIGHTFUL LAPIS LAZULI

### THE TRUTH SEEKER

A stone that promotes clarity and deep thinking, lapis lazuli helps us pursue knowledge and truth. It encourages objectivity and stimulates peace. A great companion for enhancing learning and quick thinking.

## Inspired Labradorite

### THE IDEA GENERATOR

Thought to enhance intuition and creativity, this stone encourages out-of-the-box thinking. It's perfect for brainstorming new ideas or problem-solving in class.

## MINDFUL AMETHYST

### THE PEACEFUL WARRIOR

Considered a tool for meditation and mindfulness, this stone helps promote balance and inner strength. It helps us stay calm and generates peace. Good for helping to solve quibbles or clear the mind.

## Courageous Tiger's Eye
**THE DECISION MAKER**

Known to instill confidence and bravery, helping us make good choices, especially in tough situations or doubtful moments. It's a reminder to trust your instincts and stay strong.

## Creative Garnet
**THE IMAGINATION BOOSTER**

This stone encourages imaginative thinking and artistic expression. It's connected to building confidence and overcoming creative blocks, making it easier to dream up stories, or make awesome creations.

## Focused Jade
**A LUCKY CHARM AND STUDY BUDDY**

A symbol of good fortune, said to promote harmony, calm, and stability. Believed to help with maintaining focus—useful for heavy homework and managing difficult tasks!

## Compassionate Rose Quartz
**THE FRIENDSHIP BUILDER**

Known as the "stone of love," rose quartz is said to nurture love and kindness, which can strengthen friendships and promote self-acceptance. It encourages us to be empathetic and supportive toward others.

## Motivating Amber
**THE MEMORY AND MOOD BOOSTER**

Amber is often considered an ancient shield, with stress-relieving properties that aid memory and help keep us organized. It embodies warmth and encouragement, boosting self-confidence and keeping us ready for anything!

## Optimistic Peridot
**THE HAPPINESS ENHANCER**

A glowing stone that promotes positivity, creativity, and resilience. It helps us manage stress in friendships and fosters a sense of abundance and joy. It's also said to work against nightmares!

## Serene Aquamarine
**THE STRESS REDUCER**

Historically used to protect sailors and bring good fortune, this stone is linked to relaxation and mental clarity, and can help ease anxiety before tests or life events big and small.

# April DIAMOND

# April DIAMOND

Emily P. Wheeler diamond "Riviere" necklace

April sparklers, your birthstone is the diamond—a symbol of strength, purity, clarity, and abundance. These dazzling gems form deep in Earth's mantle, nearly 100 miles below the surface, and hitch a ride to the upper crust through rare volcanic formations called kimberlites. Diamonds have long been a popular choice for engagement rings, as a symbol of love and commitment, and were once considered divine blessings from the gods. Today, diamonds outsell every other gemstone—they are treasured for their beauty, their ability to be cut and faceted to capture light, and their geological significance. There is no gemstone quite like a diamond!

## Haha!

**Why do bunnies love diamonds?**

*All the carats!*

## Fun Fact!

**Most diamonds were formed between 1 billion and 3 billion years ago!**

Bulgari diamond "Serpenti" necklace

Diamond and emerald frog

Jemma Wynne diamond and yellow gold ring

## Color Spectrum

**Diamonds come in many different colors, including pink, blue, yellow, green, and even black. The rarest color for a diamond is red.**

Van Cleef & Arpels diamond and gold "Zip" necklace

# Symbolism & Meaning

**Purity, innocence, and eternal love**

**Believed to help ease emotional pain, provide mental clarity, and bring prosperity**

# Fun Fact!

**Only about 30% of the diamonds mined worldwide are classified as gem quality.**

Marlo Laz diamond and yellow gold ring

Glenn Spiro diamond earrings

Briony Raymond diamond and yellow gold ring

Mikimoto diamond ring

# Specs

| CHEMICAL COMPOSITION | HARDNESS |
|---|---|
| Carbon | 10 on the Mohs' scale (the hardest natural mineral) |

# Diamond's 4 Cs: Learning About Cut, Color, Clarity, and Carat Weight

In the 1940s, gemologist Robert Shipley sparkled up the diamond industry with his brilliant "4Cs." Until then, comparing diamonds was a head-scratching puzzle for both experts and buyers. This clever system quickly became the universal language for diamond quality and value.

## 1. CUT

### THE SPARKLING SYMPHONY

Behold the first C: cut! Imagine a diamond as a tiny sparkling symphony—the cut is the conductor guiding every facet to play with the light. Discover how different cuts create various shapes, each with their own personality and sparkle. See pages 42–43 for more!

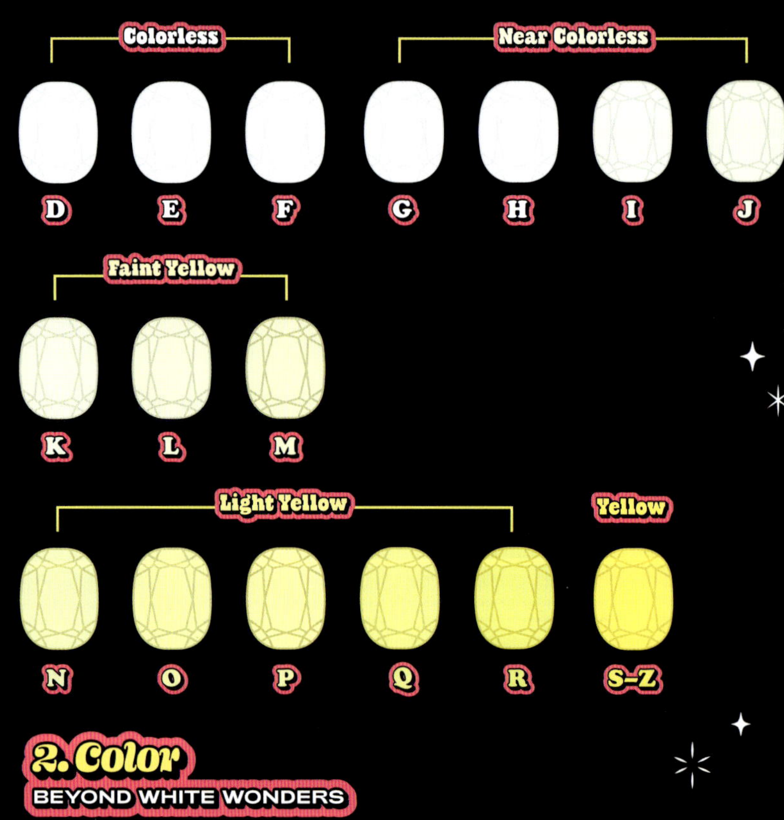


## 2. Color

### BEYOND WHITE WONDERS

Explore the second C: color! While diamonds are often known for their white (aka colorless!) brilliance, did you know they come in a rainbow of colors? From rare reds and pinks caused by Earth's pressure to yellows caused by nitrogen, each hue, including elusive orange and mysterious black, tells a unique story of the diamond's formation deep within our planet. See pages 46–47 for color charts!

## 3. CLARITY

### FINDING THE DIAMOND'S INNER SPARKLE

Clarity is the third C, and it's all about a diamond's secrets. Diamonds tell a story through their clarity, showing tiny "birthmarks" called inclusions that formed as the gem grew. Special magnifying glasses can spot these tiny features, grading diamonds from super clear "Flawless" all the way to "Imperfect," with each level revealing a unique chapter in the diamond's journey to your jewelry box.

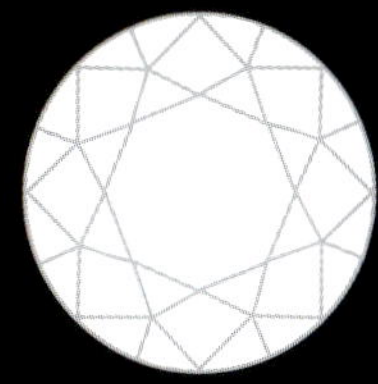

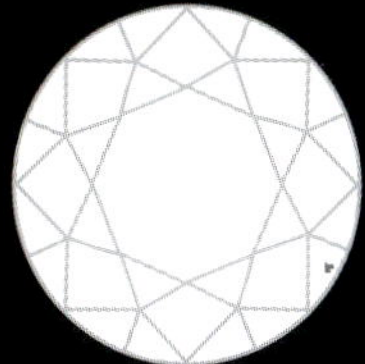

IF
INTERNALLY FLAWLESS

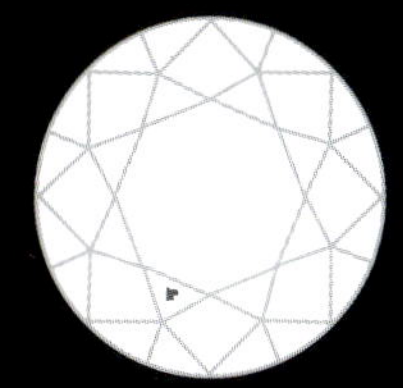

VVS1-VVS2
VERY VERY SLIGHT INCLUSIONS

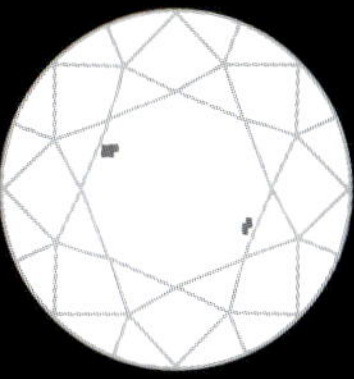

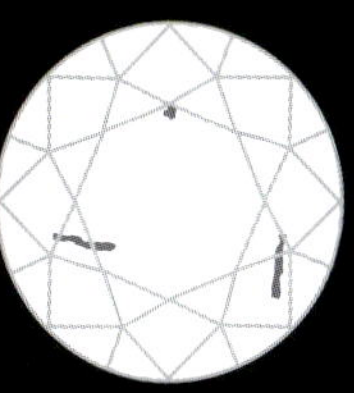

SI1-SI2
SLIGHT INCLUSIONS

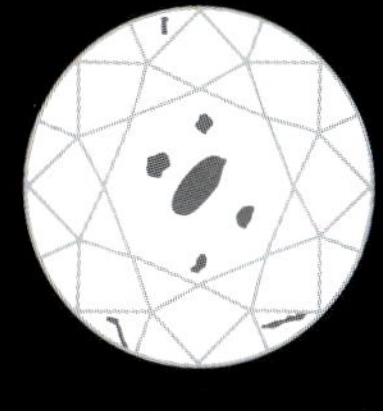

I1-SI3
IMPERFECT

Did you know the word carat comes from carob seeds? Ancient gem traders used these seeds to weigh precious stones because of their consistent size. That simple seed inspired the carat system we still use today!

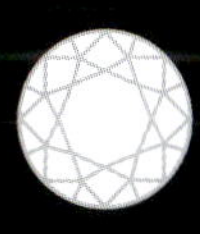

0.25CT
4.1MM

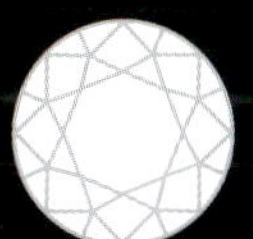

0.50CT
5.2MM

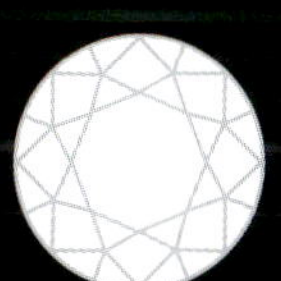

0.75CT
5.9MM

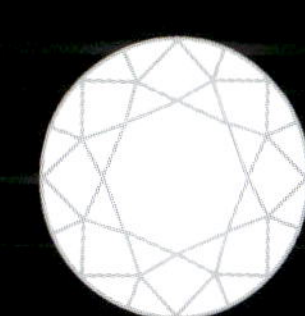

1.00CT
6.5MM

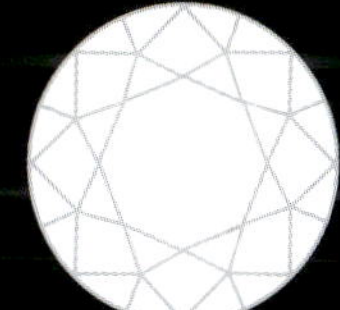

1.50CT
7.4MM

## 4. CARAT WEIGHT

### THE SIZE ADVENTURE

Carat the fourth C, is all about a diamond's weight, not its size. Gemologists use super-precise scales that can measure to hundredths of a gram.One carat equals 0.2 grams, about the same weight as a paper clip! Bigger isn't always better, though—a smaller diamond with excellent cut, color, and clarity can outshine a larger one.

2.00CT
8.2MM

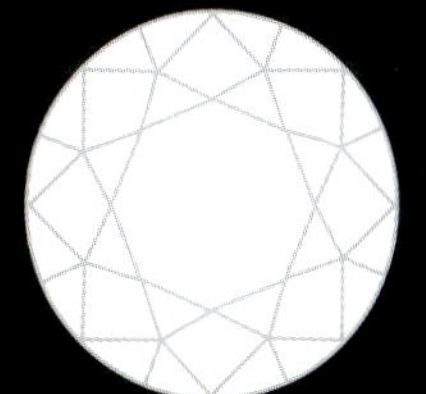

2.50CT
9.0MM

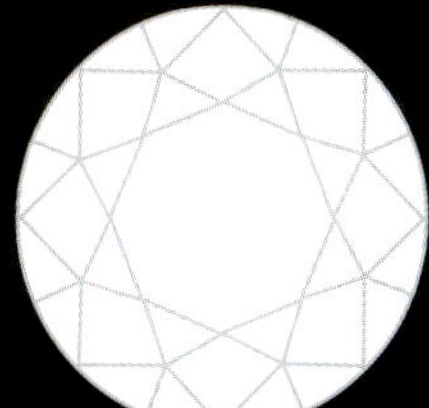

3.00CT
9.3MM

# Diamond Brilliance: The Science of Sparkle

Diamonds are marvels of nature, each one with its own unique structure that determines its beauty and value. From the sparkling surface to the hidden depths, every part of a diamond plays a role in creating its dazzling appearance. The crown, pavilion, and facets work together to bend and reflect light, while inclusions tell the story of the gem's formation. Understanding these elements reveals the science behind this gemstone's brilliance and helps us appreciate its true wonder.

**Fun Fact!**

The part of a gem that wraps around its middle is called the girdle. It's like the gem's belt, holding the top and bottom together!

## Anatomy of a Diamond

1. Star Length
2. Table Size
3. Girdle Thickness
4. Crown Height
5. Total Depth
6. Crown Angle
7. Pavilion Depth
8. Culet
9. Pavilion Angle
10. Lower Girdle

# How Diamonds Dazzle: A Look Inside

Picture light as a tiny explorer zooming through a diamond. The stone's structure and cut determine the light's path and the dazzle it throws off.

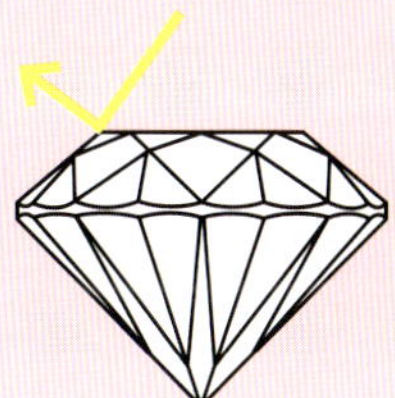

### THE BOUNCE (REFLECTION)

Some light hits the diamond and goes "Nope!," bouncing right off. That's the first flash you see. In science-speak, we call this *external reflection.*

### THE BEND (REFRACTION)

Light that makes it inside the diamond begins to twist and bend. It's like the diamond is a funhouse mirror for light rays! This bending of light is called *refraction.*

### THE PINBALL GAME (INTERNAL REFLECTION)

Once inside, light bounces around like an intense game of pinball. Scientists call this cool effect *total internal reflection.*

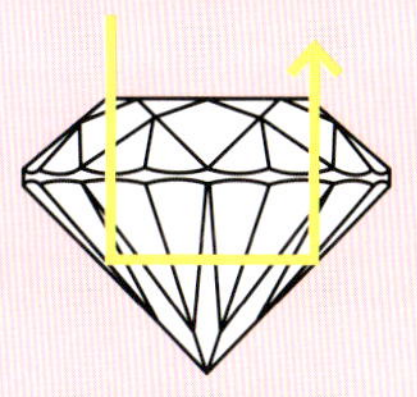

### THE RAINBOW FACTORY (DISPERSION)

As light zooms through, it splits into all the colors of the rainbow. That's why you see those awesome flashes of color. The fancy term for this is *dispersion.*

### THE DISCO BALL EFFECT (SCINTILLATION)

All this bouncing and bending creates a nonstop light show as you move the diamond around. Gemologists call this sparkly effect *scintillation.*

## Crowning Glory
### CROWN AND TABLE

Every gem has its own crowning glory—the crown and table! It's right at the top of the gem, where facets meet to create a dazzling display. When looking at a gem for the first time, pay attention to how the crown and table work together to catch and reflect light, turning a gem into a brilliant star!

## The Magical Core
### GEMSTONE INCLUSIONS

Inclusions are sometimes seen as defects or impurities, but in actuality, they are a gem's fingerprints, each telling the unique tale of the gem's journey through the earth. Foreign substances or internal features, commonly called inclusions, can be enclosed within a gem as it forms over time. These unique characteristics create tiny secret worlds inside each gem!

## THE SPARKLING HEART
### PAVILION AND CULET

A pavilion reflects light back through the crown, enhancing brilliance, while the culet at its base can either add facets or create risk of chipping, depending on its shape. A pointed culet maximizes sparkle but is more fragile!

## Facet Fun
### THE MANY FACES OF A GEM

Gems love to show off! Facets are the many faces of a gem. Each facet is a flat surface that catches light and creates a symphony of brilliance. The crown facets on top direct light into the gem, while the pavilion facets at the bottom bounce it back up, creating a brilliant dance of light that makes the stone come alive.

Be like a
DIAMOND

TOUGH,
BRILLIANT,
and made to
SHINE
no matter the
pressure

# Rainbow Radiance: Diamond Color Spectrum

When we think of diamonds, we usually envision a colorless stone, reflecting rainbows of light. But colored diamonds—no surprise here!—are some of the most jaw-dropping, colorful stones Mother Nature creates and among the most valuable, too—reds and blues are among the MOST rare and most expensive!

Fun Fact!
Tiffany & Co. used a yellow diamond in their advertising campaign in the 1970s, which helped to popularize yellow diamonds as a gemstone.

# May

# Emerald

# May Emerald

May muses, your birthstone is the emerald—a gem as green and vibrant as a lush jungle! Emeralds are a lucky charm that bring harmony and happiness and help their wearers to see the beauty in everything. These gemstones are aligned with truth and intelligence, believed to confer superpowers like wisdom, patience, and unconditional love. Did you know that emeralds were once thought to keep you safe from evil spirits? The emerald is also a symbol of loyalty and faithfulness, and some believe it has healing powers.

Bulgari emerald and diamond ring

**LOL!**

**What do you call a group of emeralds that play music together?**

A rock band!

## Fun Fact!

**The world's largest single rough emerald, the Bahia Emerald, weighs approximately 836 pounds—that's about the size of an adult polar bear!**

## Color Spectrum

**Emeralds are part of the beryl family. Their unique composition includes chromium or vanadium, which cause them to develop a green color.**

*Tiara belonging to the Duchesse d'Angoulême, given as a gift by Louis XVIII*

Van Cleef & Arpels emerald, ruby, and diamond humming bird brooches

Bulgari emerald necklace (famously worn by actress Elizabeth Taylor)

## Symbolism & Meaning

**Hopeful and uplifting, offering inspiration and balance**

**Believed to promote friendship, peace, and harmony, and to enable the wearer to both give and receive unconditional love**

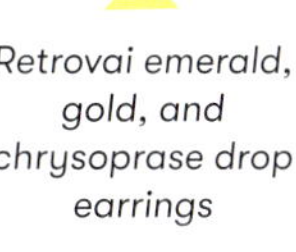

Retrovai emerald, gold, and chrysoprase drop earrings

Reza emerald, diamond, and rose and white gold "Frame" ring

## Fun Fact!

**Queen Cleopatra claimed ownership of all emerald mines in Egypt during her reign. *(For a related plot twist, read up on peridot on page 76!)***

## Specs

| CHEMICAL COMPOSITION | HARDNESS |
| --- | --- |
| Beryl with traces of chromium or vanadium | 7.5–8 on the Mohs' scale |

— IRIS APFEL

# Star Signs: Constellations and Crystals

Every birthday is unique and filled with wonder and promise. Birthstones are the guardians and physical symbols of that special energy. Each sparkling gemstone is cosmically linked to exactly when you were born, so its meaning and connection to you is truly written in the stars!

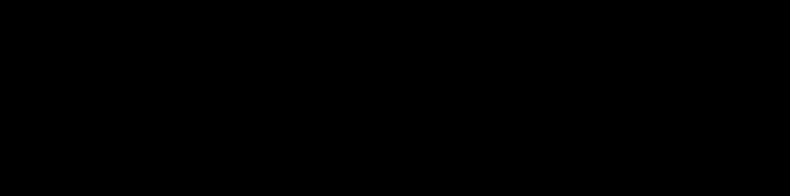

## Aquarius

**DATES**
Jan. 20 – Feb. 18

**ELEMENT**
Air

**CHARACTERISTICS**

- insightful
- innovative
- eccentric
- creative
- original

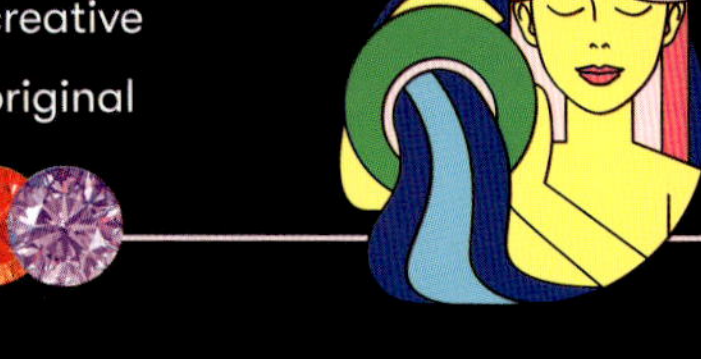

## Pisces

**DATES**
Feb. 19 – Mar. 20

**ELEMENT**
Water

**CHARACTERISTICS**

- imaginative
- compassionate
- deep
- intuitive
- empathetic

## Aries

**DATES**
Mar. 21 – Apr. 19

**ELEMENT**
Fire

**CHARACTERISTICS**

- brave
- creative
- determined
- honest
- adventurous

## Leo

**DATES**
Jul. 23 – Aug. 22

**ELEMENT**
Fire

**CHARACTERISTICS**

- regal
- faithful
- generous
- imaginative
- confident

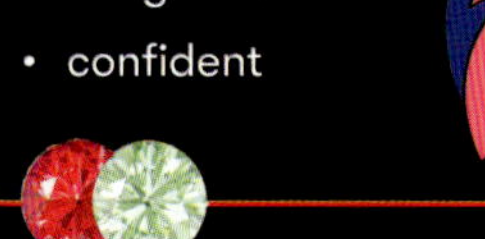

## Virgo

**DATES**
Aug. 23 – Sept. 22

**ELEMENT**
Earth

**CHARACTERISTICS**

- reflective
- hardworking
- observant
- softhearted
- smart

## Libra

**DATES**
Sept. 23 – Oct. 22

**ELEMENT**
Air

**CHARACTERISTICS**

- balanced
- compassionate
- artistic
- diplomatic
- visionary

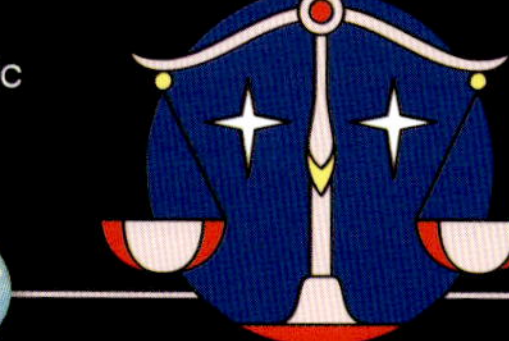

## Taurus

| DATES | ELEMENT |
| --- | --- |
| Apr. 20 – May 20 | Earth |

**CHARACTERISTICS**

- loyal
- sophisticated
- patient
- affectionate
- calm

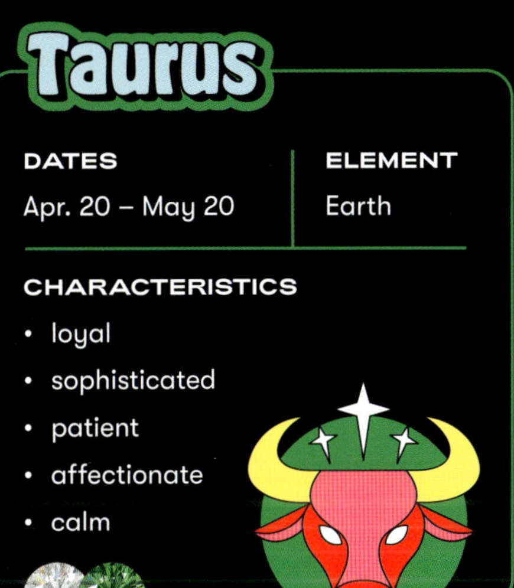

## Gemini

| DATES | ELEMENT |
| --- | --- |
| May 21 – Jun. 20 | Air |

**CHARACTERISTICS**

- social
- intelligent
- communicative
- adaptable
- charming

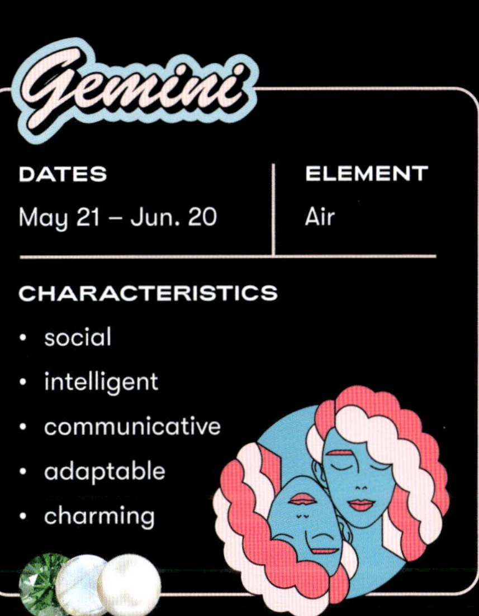

## Cancer

| DATES | ELEMENT |
| --- | --- |
| Jun. 21 – Jul. 22 | Water |

**CHARACTERISTICS**

- emotional
- outgoing
- nurturing
- intuitive
- enterprising

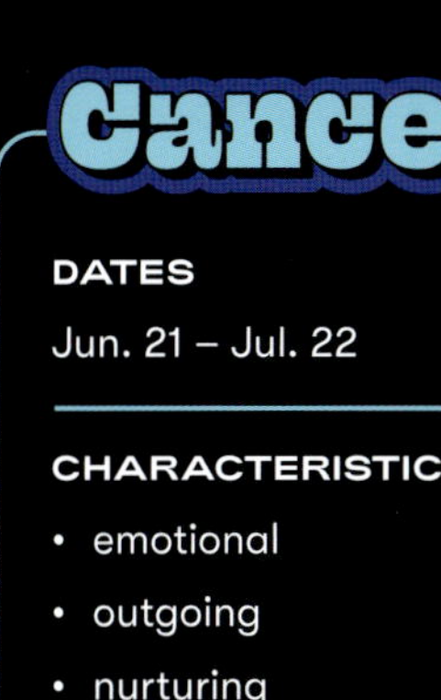

## Scorpio

| DATES | ELEMENT |
| --- | --- |
| Oct. 23 – Nov. 21 | Water |

**CHARACTERISTICS**

- purposeful
- strong-willed
- perceptive
- passionate
- curious

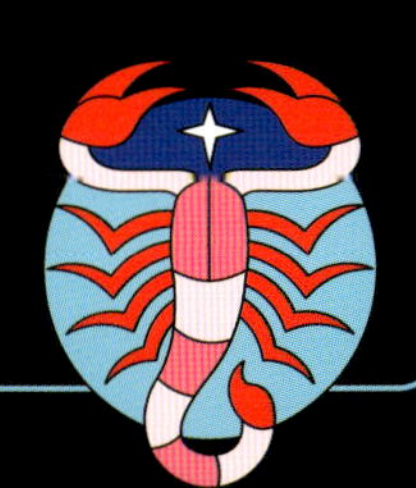

## Sagittarius

| DATES | ELEMENT |
| --- | --- |
| Nov. 22 – Dec. 21 | Fire |

**CHARACTERISTICS**

- optimistic
- honest
- festive
- free-spirited
- energetic

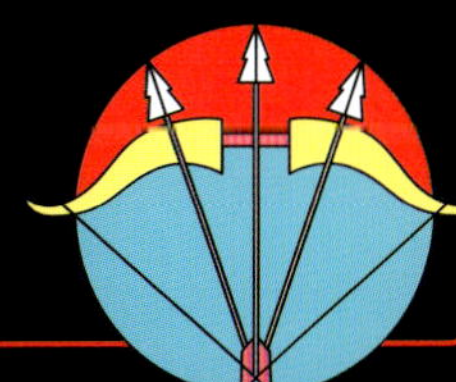

## Capricorn

| DATES | ELEMENT |
| --- | --- |
| Dec. 22 – Jan. 19 | Earth |

**CHARACTERISTICS**

- responsible
- ambitious
- steady
- patient
- willful

## June

# Pearl & Moonstone

# June Pearl

June treasures, did you know that your birthstone is a pearl? Pearls are special gemstones made by mollusks including marine oysters and freshwater mussels. Yep, you heard that right—pearls are formed inside a living animal! These beautiful glistening gems, which are said to bring luck and inner peace, have been considered a symbol of purity and innocence for thousands of years. Pearls were once believed to be tears of the gods and were considered more valuable than diamonds!

**Lol!**

**Why don't oysters share their pearls?**

They're too shell-fish.

**Fun Fact!**

**Pearls are the only gemstones that are formed by living creatures.**

*Harry Winston pearl earrings*

*Seaman Schepps baroque pearl, diamond, and sapphire bird brooch*

## Color Spectrum

**Pearls come in a variety of colors ranging from whites and creams to pinks, blues, and even black!**

## Symbolism & Meaning

**Purity, integrity, and self-awareness**

**Believed to bring good luck, wisdom, and emotional balance**

*Ella Gafter pearl, diamond, rock crystal, and white and yellow gold corsage brooch*

*Sophie Bille Brahe Botticelli pearl earrings*

*Mikimoto pearl and diamond collar*

*Mikimoto classic white South Sea cultured pearl and diamond necklace*

## Specs

| CHEMICAL COMPOSITION | HARDNESS |
| --- | --- |
| Calcium carbonate, conchiolin, and water | 2.5–4.5 on the Mohs' scale |

The
PEARL
is the
Queen
of GEMS

# and the GEM of QUEENS

— GRACE KELLY

Pearl Paradise:

# A Sea of Treasures *and* Secrets

defense. Each stunning gem is created when a mollusk responds to an irritant like a grain of sand entering its shell and coats the tiny intruder with nacre, a shiny substance repeatedly, for months or even years until a pearl is formed.

## Fun Fact!

Natural pearls found in their wild habitat are extremely rare. The odds of an oyster in the wild producing a gem-grade quality pearl are only 1 in 10,000!

### Conch Pearl

FORMED IN THE QUEEN CONCH MOLLUSK

Most famous ones come in other-worldly pink tones. The very finest conch pearls have a burst of light, a swirl or a flame-like pattern that makes them highly prized. Because conch shells are so curvy, it's tricky to find the pearls inside. They are often discovered when people eat the conch meat and open the shell to eat the conch meat—behold a true treasure!

### MELO MELO PEARL

PRODUCED BY THE MELO MELO SEA SNAIL

Golden, bright-orange colored with a sunburst-like pattern. They are extremely rare and take extremely long (decades!) to grow to a decent size.

### Quahog Clam Pearl

PRODUCED IN A CLAM

Their surface is smooth and often shows flame or honeycomb patterns. Each pearl is one of a kind, with the purple hues being the most prized. Historically, these special pearls were used by Native Americans to craft wampum , beads that held monetary and cultural value.

### Spiny Oyster Pearl

FROM THE SPINY, OR "THORNY," OYSTER

These pearls have flame-like patterns and are white, cream, pink, orange, brown, or purple. Bonus fact: The spiny oyster is actually technically a scallop!

## Natural Pearls

## Sea of Cortez Pearl

**FARMED ON A SINGLE PEARL FARM IN GUYAMAS, MEXICO**

Cultured pearls from the Sea of Cortez (aka the Gulf of California) are the rarest in the world, with fewer than 5,000 pearls produced each year.

These pearls are like underwater rainbows, showing off a dazzling array of colors, from ocean blues and forest greens to shimmering silvers and rich golds. They even have secret hues of violet and black, and best of all, these pearls have a hidden superpower! Under special UV light, they transform into glowing treasures, lighting up in pink or red!

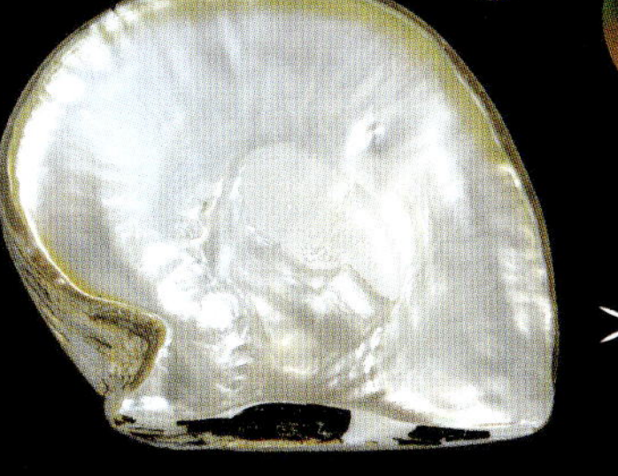

## South Sea Pearl

**WHITE ONES: PRIMARILY CULTIVATED IN AUSTRALIA AND INDONESIA**

**GOLDEN ONES: MAINLY PRODUCED IN THE PHILIPPINES AND INDONESIA**

Meet the gentle giants of the pearl world—these stunners can grow as big as your thumb! They come in gorgeous creamy white and warm golden hues, courtesy of the Pinctada maxima saltwater oyster, the largest pearl-producing oyster around, which can reach an impressive 12 inches in diameter. Silver-lipped oysters produce white pearls, while their gold-lipped friends make pearls with golden tones.

Ninety-nine percent of all South Sea pearls undergo no treatment of any kind other than a gentle washing and buffing after harvest. Their super-thick nacre coating gives them a soft, moonlit glow. Unlike their Akoya cousins, with their high-beam sparkle, South Sea pearls have a dreamy, silky shimmer that's all their own.

## TAHITIAN PEARL

**CULTURED THROUGHOUT FRENCH POLYNESIAN ISLANDS**

The Tahitian pearl oyster, *Pinctada margaritifera*, is also known as the "black lip" oyster!

This is a naturally colored black pearl, in shadowy shades like pastel dove gray and darker charcoal hues.

And here's the magic part: They have secret "overtones"—shimmery colors that dance over their dark surface like tiny rainbows on a stormy sky.

## AKOYA PEARL

**CULTURED IN JAPAN, CHINA, AND VIETNAM**

Akoya pearls usually shine in classic white, but can also surprise with silvery blue or soft golden hues. When dyed black, they transform into mysterious gems with a deep midnight blue-black glow. The most prized among them are hanadama or "flower pearls," treasured in Japan for their exceptional beauty and perfection.

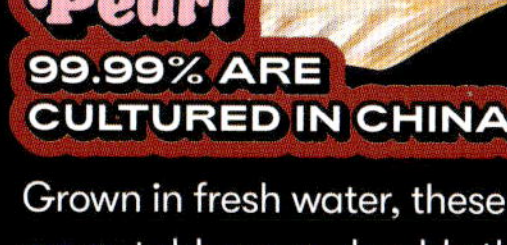

## Freshwater Pearl

**99.99% ARE CULTURED IN CHINA**

Grown in fresh water, these beauties are notably more durable than other pearls due to their unique structure. Made almost entirely of nacre, they can grow layers up to 6mm thick!

They naturally come in a variety of colors, including pastel shades of peach, pink, lavender, and white.

What's more, freshwater pearls can be dyed black, creating super-iridescent blue-green and violet hues often referred to as "peacock."

## June
# MOONSTONE

June dreamers, your birthstone is the enchanting moonstone. Shimmery, opalescent moonstones radiate an aura of mystery and grace. Throughout history, from ancient Rome to Hindu mythology, moonstones were believed to bring a sense of calm and balance. Just as the moon controls the tides, moonstones are thought to guide emotions and open the door to new beginnings. So if you're ever feeling like you need a touch of moonlit magic, press a moonstone into your palm and let the calm wash over you.

*Brent Neale rainbow moonstone, multicolored sapphire, and gold mushroom and heart pendant necklaces*

### Haha!

**How does a moonstone cut his hair?**

Eclipse it!

### Fun Fact!

**Moonstones can display a mesmerizing play of color, known as "adularescence," which gives them a magical glow.**

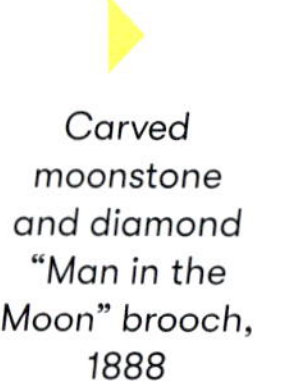

*Carved moonstone and diamond "Man in the Moon" brooch, 1888*

### COLOR SPECTRUM

**Typically white, or colorless with a blue sheen, moonstones also come in shades of peach, green, and gray.**

## Symbolism & Meaning

**Mystery, love, and new beginnings**

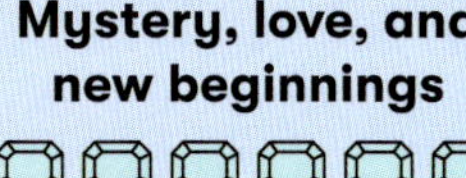

**Associated with the moon and believed to bring calm, balance, and good fortune**

*Verdura cabochon moonstone, diamond, and gold ring*

*Irene Neuwirth rainbow moonstone bracelet with yellow gold and pavé diamonds*

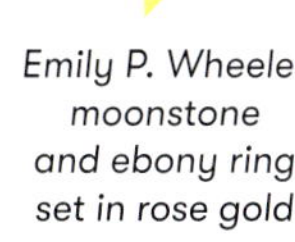

*Emily P. Wheeler moonstone and ebony ring set in rose gold*

*JAR moonstone, sapphire, and diamond ear clips*

## Fun Fact!

**Moonstones are feldspars, minerals found in Earth's crust. A variety of these minerals are also found on the surface of the actual moon!**

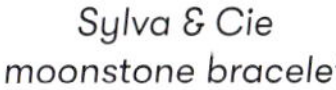

*Sylva & Cie moonstone bracelet*

## Specs

| CHEMICAL COMPOSITION | HARDNESS |
| --- | --- |
| A variety of feldspars | 6–6.5 on the Mohs' scale |

# July
# Ruby

# July Ruby

July heartthrobs, your birthstone is the ruby, a fiery gemstone that's all about passion and love! This beautiful red gem is believed to protect wearers from harm and bring good luck in love. Rubies are from the family of the mineral corundum, which also includes sapphires. In ancient times, rubies were believed to offer protection from evil and illness. Ancient warriors even implanted rubies in their skin to protect them in battle. Ouch! Ruby is a firecracker of a gemstone, full of energy and healing power. These are gemstones to help you speak your truth and go after what your heart desires.

*Van Cleef & Arpels ruby and pearl "Camellia" brooch*

## Lol!

**Why did the ruby break up with the diamond?**

It couldn't take the pressure.

## Fun Fact!

**Rubies found in Greenland are believed to be some of the oldest on the planet—approximately 3 billion years old.**

## Color Spectrum

**Rubies aren't just red—they can range from the most vivid and valuable "pigeon's blood" red to deep pink. Lighter pinks are classified as pink sapphires!**

*Retrouvai bracelet with baguette-cut rubies*

Glenn Spiro ruby necklace

Graff ruby earrings

Van Cleef & Arpels ruby and diamond necklace

Reza ruby, white gold, and diamond "Ayli" ring

Glenn Spiro cushion-cut ruby ring

## Symbolism & Meaning

**Love, passion, and courage**

**Believed to enhance energy, promote health, and increase motivation**

## Specs

| CHEMICAL COMPOSITION | HARDNESS |
|---|---|
| Corundum with traces of chromium | 9 on the Mohs' scale |

SHINE

is my
favorite
color

— MARC JACOBS

# Nature's Brushstrokes: Discovering Earth-Made Artistry

Step into a world where gems are more than just pretty colors; they're tiny art galleries, showcasing unique patterns and secrets from below Earth's surface. These special stones tell intricate tales of their own, stories written in their lines, swirls, and mesmerizing inclusions.

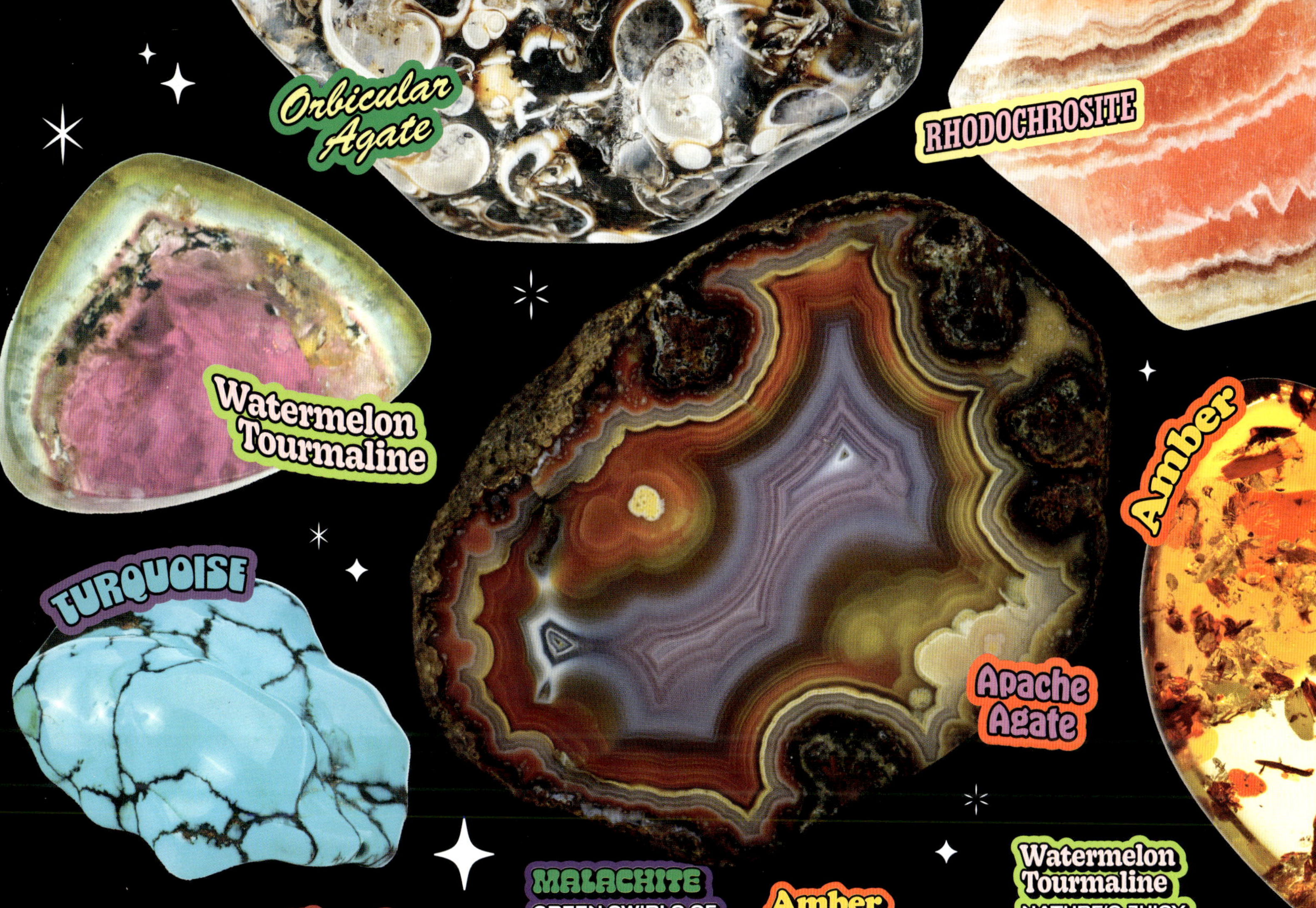


**RHODOCHROSITE**
**BURSTS OF EARTHLY LOVE**

Cutting into this marvel exposes deep pinkish shades forming banded patterns that resemble a luscious rose.

**Tiger Eye**
**GOLDEN GLIMMER**

A glimmering golden-brown stone that steals its colors from nature's biggest cats. Its mesmerizing cat-eye effect is known as chatoyancy—a silky, wavy shimmer.

**MALACHITE**
**GREEN SWIRLS OF TRANSFORMATION**

Often found in stalagmite clusters within caves, malachites feature swirls of ultra-vivid green. It's no wonder ancient Egyptians crushed them to create vivid eye makeup!

**Amber**
**ANCIENT SUNLIGHT**

Amber, formed from fossilized tree resin, glows with the warmth of ancient sunlight. These windows into the past often contain preserved insects or plant material.

**Watermelon Tourmaline**
**NATURE'S JUICY DELIGHT**

Slice into this gem and reveal a candy-like medley of colors—vivid pinks at the core, encircled by lush green edges.

**Jasper**
**NATURE'S MONET**

This gem's earthly hues show up in patterns that mimic landscapes, scenic views, even animal prints.

**LAPIS LAZULI**
**STARRY NIGHT**

An unmistakable ultramarine stone—like an Yves Klein canvas flecked with gold.

**Orbicular Agate**
**COSMIC CIRCLES**

Look closely to discover hypnotic circles, like tiny whirling planets captured in stone.

**TURQUOISE**
**HIDDEN TREASURES**

This unmistakable blue stunner is the only gemstone to have an actual color named after it.

**Apache Agate**
**EARTH'S ABSTRACT MASTERPIECE**

Forming in layers over millions of years, no two agates are ever exactly alike, even if they are cut from the same rock.

# August

# PERIDOT

# August
# PERIDOT

**A** **ugust** apples of our eye, did you know that your birthstone is the peridot? This glowing green gemstone is said to bring happiness, joy, and abundance, and to attract positive energy. In Hawaiian folklore, peridot was said to be tears of the goddess of volcanoes, Pele. Peridots form deep within Earth, like diamonds, but can also come from outer space! Maybe that's where they get some of their otherworldly glow, as well as some of their other reputed superpowers, like the ability to impart creativity, confidence, and inner strength.

**LOL!**

**Why did the peridot stop hanging out with the emerald?**

It was always green with envy!

*David Webb cushion-cut peridot turquoise, diamond, gold, platinum, and black enamel "Chromatic Cuff"*

*Cartier yellow gold and onyx "Panthère de Cartier" ring with peridot eyes*

**Fun Fact!**

**Peridot is often found inside meteorites and lava rocks.**

## Color Spectrum

**Peridot is the only gemstone that comes in just one color—green! It ranges from bright lime to deep olive, depending on its iron content.**

*Emily P. Wheeler ombre button studs with ombré pavé sapphires*

Elizabeth Locke peridot ring

*Buccellati peridot, diamond, and white and yellow gold pendant*

## Fun Fact!

**In ancient Egypt, peridot was known as the "gem of the sun."**

## Symbolism & Meaning

**Strength, protection, and healing**

**Believed to provide spiritual renewal, alleviate anxiety, and promote creativity**

*FoundRae peridot pear, gold, and pavé diamond medallion pendant*

*Irene Neuwirth tropical peridot flower duet ring*

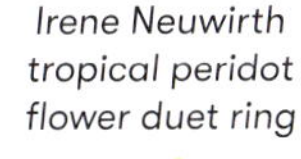

*Marlo Laz "Starburst" charm peridot necklace*

## Specs

| CHEMICAL COMPOSITION | HARDNESS |
|---|---|
| Magnesium iron silicate | 6.5–7 on the Mohs' scale |

*Giant Gems:*

# Unveiling the Biggest, Priciest, *and most* Unique Gems

## THE PINK PERFECTION DIAMOND

### A PRETTY-IN-PINK MARVEL

This dazzling gem—known as the "Eternal Pink"—weighs in at 10.57 carats, about the size of a plump grape. With its flawless interior and a color so vivid it catches every eye, this rosy marvel shattered records as the most valuable pink diamond ever sold at auction.

## GOLDEN JUBILEE DIAMOND

### A JAW-DROPPING JUMBO JEWEL

This 545-carat yellow-brown sparkler was discovered in 1985 in South Africa, hiding in the same mine that produced other famous diamonds like the Cullinan. Weighing as much as a bag of sugar and bigger than any other cut gem in the world, it took gemologists two years in a special underground room to cut the diamond. It was later gifted to the king of Thailand and now rests like a sleeping giant in Bangkok's royal museum.

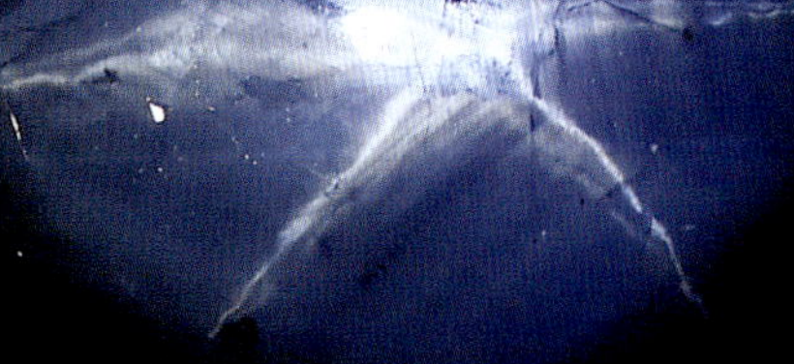

## THE STAR OF ADAM

### A SUPERSIZE STAR SAPPHIRE

It's as big as aan oversize egg and holds the title for being the largest star sapphire ever found. This galactic gem was discovered in Sri Lanka and is said to be around 400 million years old! When it was uncovered in 2015, it didn't just break the record for the largest star sapphire—it nearly DOUBLED it.

## The Empress of Uruguay

### AN ABSOLUTELY AWESOME AMETHYST

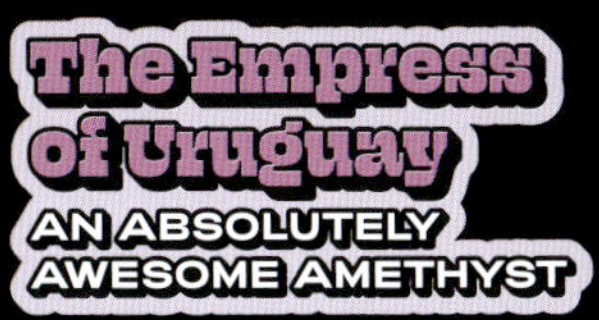

This sparkling purple geode discovered in 2007 stands at almost 11 feet (taller than a basketball hoop) and weighs 2.5 tons, making it heavier than a full-grown rhinoceros! It actually took 3 months to extract it from the solid rock around it, and it is now displayed at the Crystal Caves Museum in Atherton, Australia—where visitors are encouraged to touch it!

## THE FANTASTIC FURA EMERALD

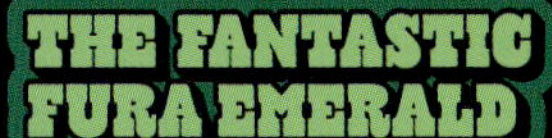

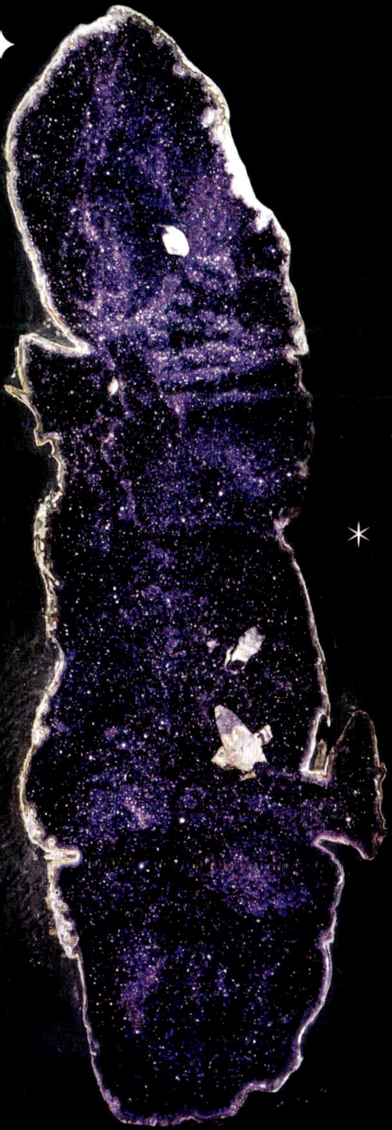

### AN AMAZING GREEN GIANT

Legend has it that a colossal emerald was unearthed deep in the heart of Colombia in the late 1990s. Known as the Fura Emerald, it reportedly boasts a size that rivals that of a juicy pineapple, with some accounts suggesting it weighs over 10,000 carats.

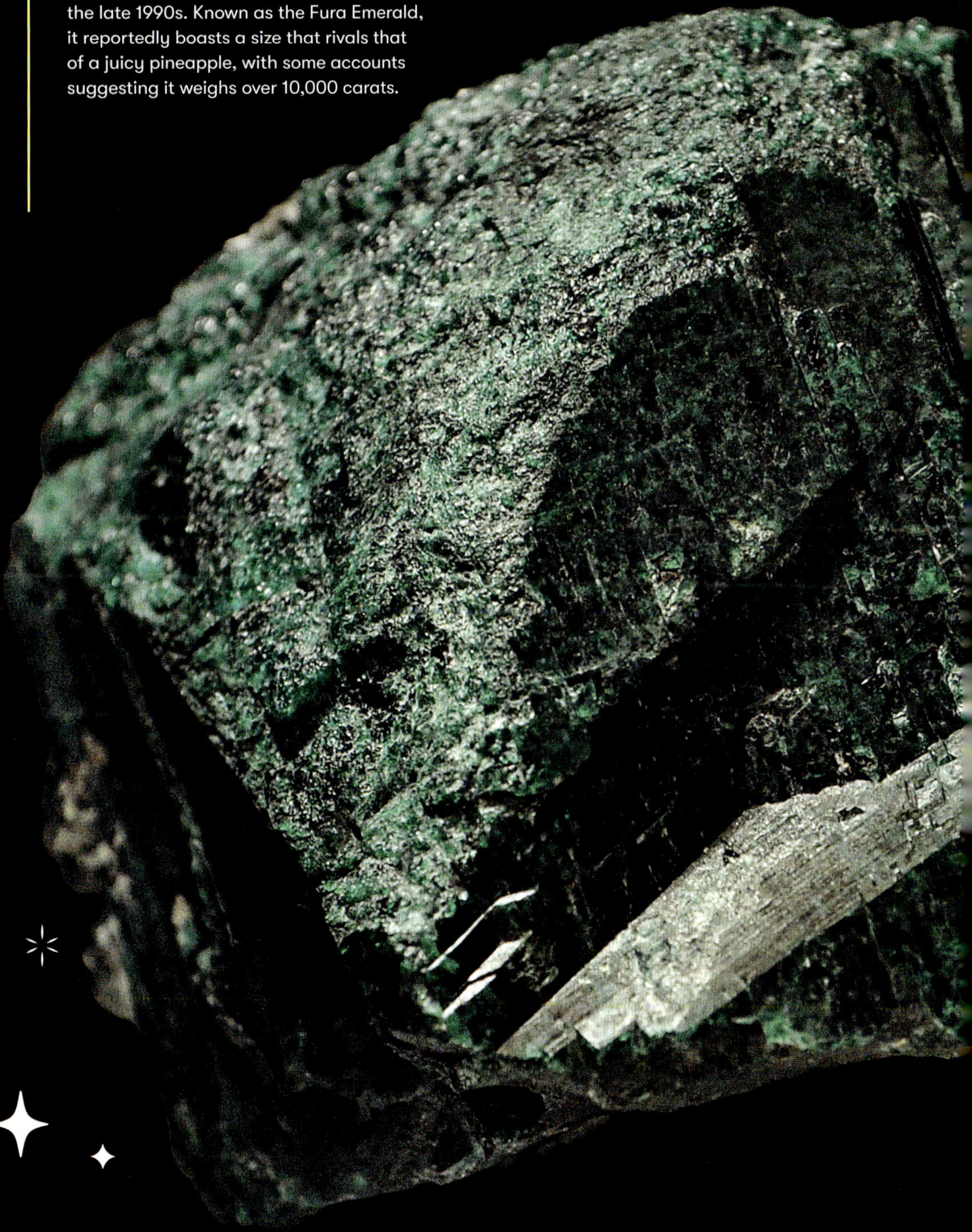

# GEMS are the silent bridges

# between ART and nature

# September SAPPHIRE

# September SAPPHIRE

**September** sages, your birthstone is the regal sapphire, a gemstone of wisdom and truth. These magnificent blue gems have been used in jewelry for thousands of years and were favored by kings and queens as a symbol of power that could protect them from envy and harm. Sapphires reminded ancient people so much of the blue sky, they once imagined that a huge sapphire not only held up Earth but also gave the sky its color. (As it turns out, this is not the case.) Still, this wise owl of a gemstone may offer its wearer clarity, spiritual enlightenment, and some inner peace. That's one powerful gem!

## Haha!

**Why did the sapphire go to the doctor?**

It was feeling a little blue.

*Glenn Spiro sapphire necklace*

*Cartier sapphire, diamond, emerald, and onyx "Panthère" ring*

## Color Spectrum

**Sapphires aren't just blue—they come in almost every color of the rainbow, including pink, yellow, and even green!**

## Fun Fact!

**Due to their incredible toughness and scratch resistance, Sapphires are now used to make phone screens, watch faces, even LED lights!**

*Tiffany & Co. sapphire, emerald, and diamond butterfly brooch*

## Symbolism & Meaning

**Wisdom, truth, and loyalty**

**Believed to promote good health, bring inner peace, and improve mental clarity**

*Briony Raymond oval-cut sapphire and diamond ring*

## Fun Fact!

**A sapphire is so strong that it can only be scratched by a diamond or another sapphire.**

*Irene Neuwirth sapphire and pavé diamond earrings*

*Marlo Laz sapphire and diamond "Alexandra" necklace*

## Specs

| CHEMICAL COMPOSITION | HARDNESS |
|---|---|
| Corundum with trace amounts of iron, titanium, or chromium | 9 on the Mohs' scale |

*Reza sapphire "Triptych" earrings*

# Beyond Blue: A Sapphire Color Wheel

The word *sapphire* is derived from the Latin word *saphirus* and the Greek word *sapheiros*, both meaning blue. And, sure enough, when we describe a gem as a sapphire, we're talking about a brilliant blue jewel from the corundum family. But, as you're about to see, sapphires come in many colors—in fact, almost EVERY color!

Non-blue sapphires are referred to as "fancy sapphires," with the exception of black and colorless ones. The only color a sapphire doesn't come in? Red. That's because we already have a name for a red corundum: ruby!

Sapphires—like diamonds—take millions of years to form within Earth. When a mineral called aluminum oxide—aka corundum—is exposed to intense pressure and heat below Earth's surface, it turns to liquid, which then seeps into cracks in metamorphic or magma-made rocks. As the liquid mineral cools, it is transformed into crystals. The color magic happens when a tiny trace of another mineral manages to mix in with the corundum—resulting in colors like pink, violet, yellow, and blue!

Fun Fact!
Bicolor sapphires appear to show two different colors under the same lighting conditions—a single stone can be salmon and yellow, or teal and light green, or blue and purple, and so on!
It's a two-fer! Some sapphires are known for their very rare color effects. Color-change sapphires appear blue in sunlight and purple-y under artificial light.

Jewels are reminders from nature that

beauty

DEEP

is found
WITHIN

# October
# OPAL & PINK TOURMALINE

**October** optimists, your birthstone is the opal, a unique gem that symbolizes hope, creativity, and love. Opals reflect all the colors of the rainbow and were once believed to help people see into the future. Ancient Romans saw opals as a symbol of hope and purity. These shimmering rainbow gems are believed to help wearers express their individuality—increasing inspiration, intuition, and imagination. Frankly, we've never met a more mystical-looking gem.

## COLOR SPECTRUM

**Opals come in many variations, with names that describe their color, such as fire opal, a bright red variation, and island sunset opal (sunset-y!).**

*Harwell Godfrey opal necklace*

### LOL!

**How did the opal do on her rainbow exam?**

She passed with flying colors!

**Opals form when silica-rich water seeps into rock cracks and hardens over millions of years.**

*Pierre Baltensberger opal and diamond brooch*

*Monica Rich Kosann opal frog ring*

Sylva & Cie opal necklace

## Symbolism & Meaning

**Creativity, inspiration, and confidence**

**Believed to enhance emotional balance, strengthen the immune system, and promote restful sleep**

*Oscar Heyman opal swan brooch*

*Buccellati yellow and white gold, ruby, sapphire, and emerald pendant*

*David Webb opal cabochon" Notre Dame" cuff*

## Specs

| CHEMICAL COMPOSITION | HARDNESS |
|---|---|
| Hydrated silicon dioxide | 5.5–6.5 on the Mohs' scale |

OPALS:
reminding us
THAT BEING
a little
DIFFERENT

just makes you
MORE
magical!

# Kaleidoscope Gems: Revealing the Magic of Opals

Opal's magical effects come from the gem's very special inner structure: a weblike network of tiny silica spheres. As light travels through the opal, it bounces off these spheres, splitting into endless colors. That's why opal is nicknamed the "Gem of Rainbows."

Opals come in a variety of types, each with its own special look and character:

## Pink Opals

With a soft, calming color, these stones are often found in Peru and are said to be connected to Pachamama, an ancient Inca goddess whose name means "Mother Earth." They are believed to bring peace and love.

## JELLY/WATER OPALS

Found in Mexico, Australia, and the Czech Republic, their gel-like appearance and high water content (up to 30%!) showcase colors that seem to swim inside the stone!

## Crystal Opals

Transparent or translucent, crystal opals are like enchanted windows filled with shimmering rainbows. They're treasured for their vibrant color displays, set against a clear or light-colored backdrop, and are sourced from diverse locations including as Australia and Ethiopia.

## White Opals

These opals have a soft, creamy-white background with pastel flashes of color, much like a dreamy watercolor painting. They are the most abundant and widespread type of precious opal and are primarily found in Australia, especially in Coober Pedy.

## BLACK OPALS

Here's a fun fact: Black opals aren't actually black! They have a dark background that makes their rainbow colors pop vividly, like a night sky filled with stars. They are highly prized and are mainly found in Lightning Ridge, Australia.

## Fun Fact!

Some opals have been found on Mars, making them one of the few gemstones discovered outside of Earth!

It takes approximately 5 million years to form just one centimeter of opal!

## HYRDOPHANE OPALS

"Hydrophane" derives from the Greek words hydro ("water") and phainein ("to appear"), because the opal's color changes when the stone is wet—magic!

## Blue Opals

In ancient Greece and Rome, blue opals were linked to the goddess Iris. They are largely found in Peru and Brazil.

## Green Opals

Found worldwide, these opals come in striking shades of emerald, yellow-green, or muted jade. Prominent mines are in Australia, Brazil, Peru, Mexico, and the US.

## Boulder Opals

Found attached to their natural rock, combining vibrant opal colors with dark ironstone to create a stunning contrast that's like a burst of sunlight on a cloudy day. They are mainly found in Australia.

## FIRE OPALS

First discovered by the Aztecs in ancient Mexico, these captivating gems come in warm, sun-like hues ranging from fiery orange to deep red. They form in volcanic regions primarily in Mexico and Brazil.

## October
# PINK TOURMALINE

**October** blossoms! Your birthstone—the delightful pink tourmaline—is a burst of floral beauty, captured in a gem. Throughout history, pink tourmaline has been associated with love and compassion, believed to hold the power of emotional healing. Wearing pink tourmaline may bring feelings of joy and inspire creativity, opening its wearer's mind and heart—akin to how a flower opens its petals to the sun. In need of a little pick-me-up? Turn to pink tourmaline and let its rosy hues lift your spirits.

**Lol!** **Why are pink tourmalines known as optimists?**

Their rosy outlooks!

*Verdura gold and pink tourmaline "Wrapped Heart" brooch*

### Fun Fact!

**Pink tourmalines are piezoelectric, meaning they can generate an electric charge when heated or rubbed.**

*Bulgari pink tourmaline ring*

### Color Spectrum

**Though these come in a variety of pinks, a favorite of many is the watermelon tourmaline, which features pink and green in the same crystal!**

*Elizabeth Locke pink tourmaline and gold ring*

Marlo Laz pink tourmaline, gold, and diamond earrings

Seaman Schepps pink tourmaline, sapphire, cultured pearl, and diamond necklace

Jemma Wynne pink tourmaline and diamond pendant

Jemma Wynne pink tourmaline necklace

## Symbolism & Meaning

**Love, compassion, and emotional healing**

**Thought to inspire creativity and promote feelings of joy**

## Fun Fact!

**Ancient Egyptians believed tourmaline stones traveled through rainbows to absorb their colors.**

## Specs

| CHEMICAL COMPOSITION | HARDNESS |
| --- | --- |
| Complex borosilicate | 7–7.5 on the Mohs' scale |

## The Mohs' Scale:

# A Gem Strength Showdown

**Fun Fact!**

The Mohs' scale was invented by a gem wizard named Friedrich Mohs in 1812, making it older than the lightbulb!

For a gemstone, hardness isn't just about being tough. In the world of gems, "hardness" specifically means how well a stone can resist scratches.

Diamond sits at the top of the Mohs' scale at 10, making it the hardest natural substance we know. But here's a cool twist: Diamonds can actually be pretty fragile! Their crystal structure makes them resistant to scratches but prone to shattering if hit the wrong way.

This is where "toughness" comes in—it's a different property that measures how well a gem resists breaking. Jade, for example, isn't as hard as diamond, but it's way tougher. It can take a hit without shattering.

### TURQUOISE

**BOLD AND DELICATE**

Turquoise is a porous stone susceptible to chemicals, impact, and even changes in temperature.

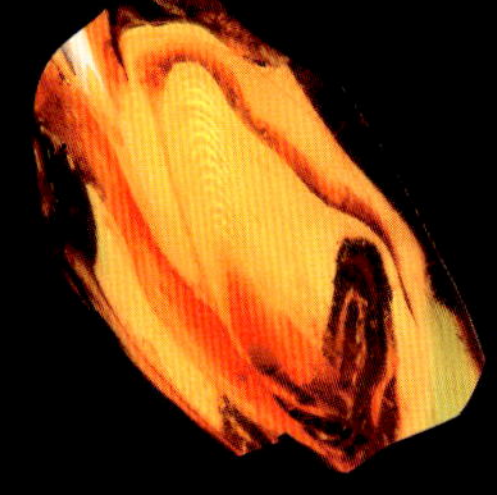

### Amber

**SENSITIVE STONES**

Amber is a soft gem that scratches easily and is reactive to heat and chemicals.

### PEARL

**PRECIOUS PALS**

These organic gems are vulnerable to acids, chemicals, and physical damage.

### Opals

**ENIGMATIC MARVELS**

Opals are delicate and can easily crack or break due to their water content and internal structure.

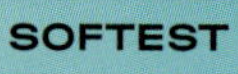

# Mohs' Scale

The Mohs' scale quantifies the hardness of each gemstone. At the lower end, the scale is more linear, with hardness moving evenly between the numbers, but at the higher end, the hardness scale climbs sharply, meaning corundum at 9 is about twice as hard as topaz at 8, and diamond at 10 is about four times as hard as corundum!

Another way to think about hardness is that each mineral on the Mohs' scale is able to scratch the ones that fall below it, and can only be scratched by the ones above it. Generally, gemstones of the same hardness won't scratch each other, with one notable exception: diamonds—and only diamonds—can scratch other diamonds.

## Quartz

### COLORFUL AND COOL UNDER PRESSURE

Rounding out the list of hardest stones, amethyst, citrine, and rose quartz are all plenty tough when it comes to withstanding daily activities.

## Topaz

### STURDY SPARKLERS

Topaz is relatively hard and resistant to scratching, making it suitable for jewelry.

## Diamonds

### RESILIENT CHAMPIONS

Known as the hardest natural substance on Earth(!), diamonds are extremely durable and resistant to scratching.

## EMERALD

### DELICATE BEAUTIES

Of the most valuable gemstones, emeralds are relatively delicate—softer than diamonds, rubies, and sapphires.

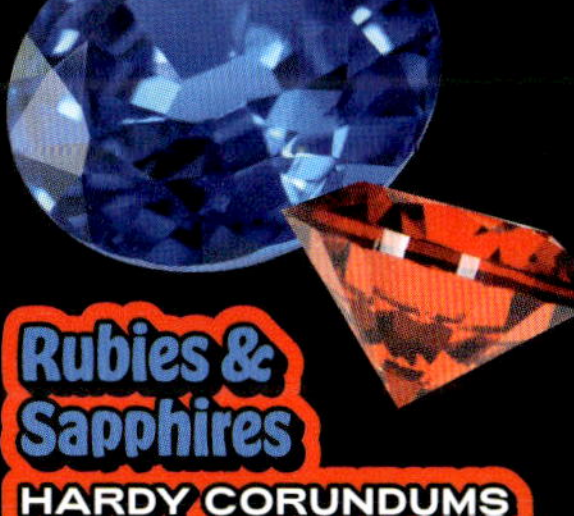

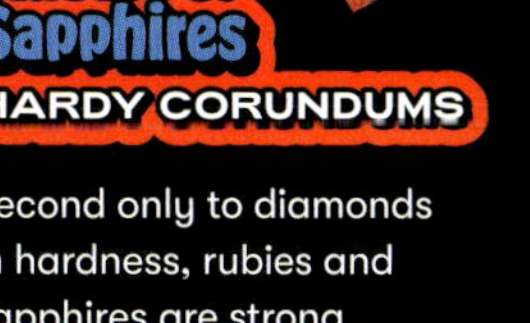

## Rubies & Sapphires

### HARDY CORUNDUMS

Second only to diamonds in hardness, rubies and sapphires are strong, durable stones that can be worn every day with little risk.

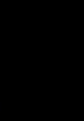

7 8 9 HARDEST 10

# November

# Citrine

# November
# Citrine

November creatives! Your birthstone is citrine, a magical gemstone tied to positivity, confidence, and success. Citrines are a burst of fresh energy, helping their wearers feel calm and creative. Soothing jewels of joy and abundance, they attract positive energy and good fortune. Citrines are naturally vibrant on their own, without any heating or other intervention by gemologists to boost their beautiful golden color. These stones are especially great for students and artists—who may feel newly creative and inspired by these crisp yellow gems.

*Material Good citrine and diamond earrings*

*JAR citrine pendant*

## Haha!

**What does a citrine need when it falls off its bike?**

Lemon-aid!

## Color Spectrum

**Citrine is from the quartz family and comes in a range of yellows, browns, and golds.**

## Fun Fact!

**Natural citrines are rare; most on the market are heat-treated amethysts or smoky quartz.**

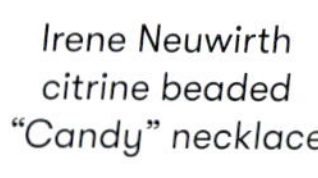

*Irene Neuwirth citrine beaded "Candy" necklace*

*Tiffany & Co. citrine, ruby, and diamond "Bird on a Rock" brooch, by Jean Schlumberger*

Buccellati yellow, white, and pink gold bangle bracelet with Madeira citrine and diamonds

Brent Neale citrine "Crown Ring" with multicolored sapphires

## Symbolism & Meaning

**Strength, wisdom, and calmness**

**Believed to bring good fortune, enhance mental clarity, and improve self-esteem**

Antique citrine and gold necklace

Marina B citrine and diamond "Gina" collar

## Specs

| CHEMICAL COMPOSITION | HARDNESS |
|---|---|
| Silicon dioxide | 7 on the Mohs' scale |

LIFE IS TO
not to
SPA

SHORT
KLE

# Legendary Gems: History's Most Famous Stones

## The Hope Diamond

A famous deep-blue diamond with a storied history, the Hope Diamond is rumored to carry a curse. It is now part of the Smithsonian's National Museum of Natural History collection. Cool fact: This blue diamond, when exposed to ultraviolet light, actually appears to glow red!

## THE DARYA-I-NOOR DIAMOND

One of the largest cut pink diamonds in the world, the Darya-i-Noor (its name means "sea of light") was discovered in India. It is now part of the Iranian Crown Jewels and is held at the Central Bank of Iran.

## The Dresden Green Diamond

Rare and historic, this 41-carat marvel is the largest natural green diamond known to exist. Believed to come from India, it has traveled plenty, even appearing in American museums alongside the Hope Diamond, and now resides in the Grünes Gewölbe (Green Vault) museum in Dresden, Germany.

## FABERGÉ EGGS

These exquisite jeweled eggs were created by the House of Fabergé for the Russian imperial family between 1885 and 1917. Each egg is a masterpiece of craftsmanship and design. Over the years, a few of the original 69 eggs have gone missing, their whereabouts a mystery!

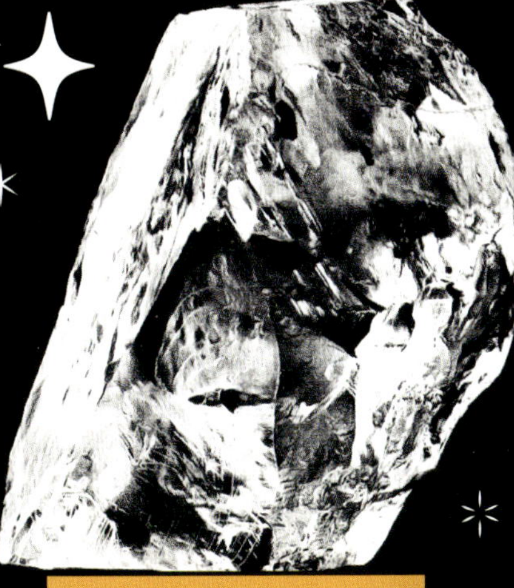

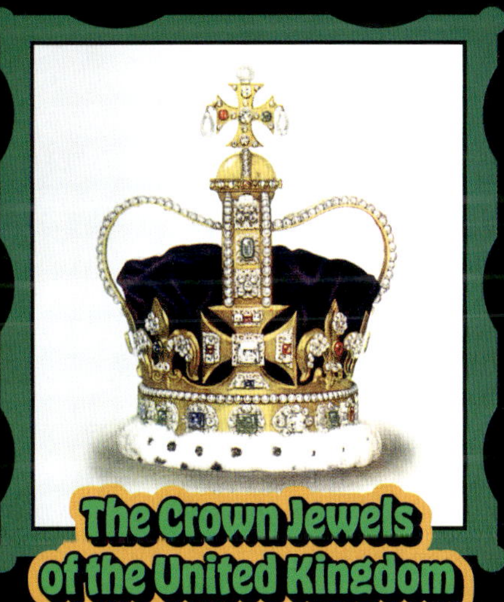


## THE KOH-I-NOOR DIAMOND

A more than 100-carat, colorless diamond, the Koh-i-Noor has a long history of ownership among various ruling dynasties in South Asia. Its name means "mountain of light," and depending on who you ask, it may be cursed! It is now part of the British Crown Jewels.

## The Cullinan Diamond

At a massive 3,106 carats, the Cullinan is the largest gem-quality diamond every discovered. It was later cut into several significant diamonds, many of which are part of the British Crown Jewels, including the Cullinan I, which—at 530.2 carats—is the largest cut diamond in the world.

## The Crown Jewels of the United Kingdom

The Crown Jewels are a spectacular group of crowns, jewelry, and royal items used for coronations and other important royal ceremonies. The collection is so valuable, it's been kept under constant guard in the Tower of London for over 600 years!

## The Great Star of Africa (Cullinan I)

The largest polished diamond cut from the Cullinan Diamond, the Great Star of Africa weighs over 500 carats and is set in the British Sovereign's Sceptre with Cross, part of the Crown Jewels. It is renowned as the largest clear-cut diamond in the world, with 74 facets of megasparkle!

# December
# Turquoise & Tanzanite

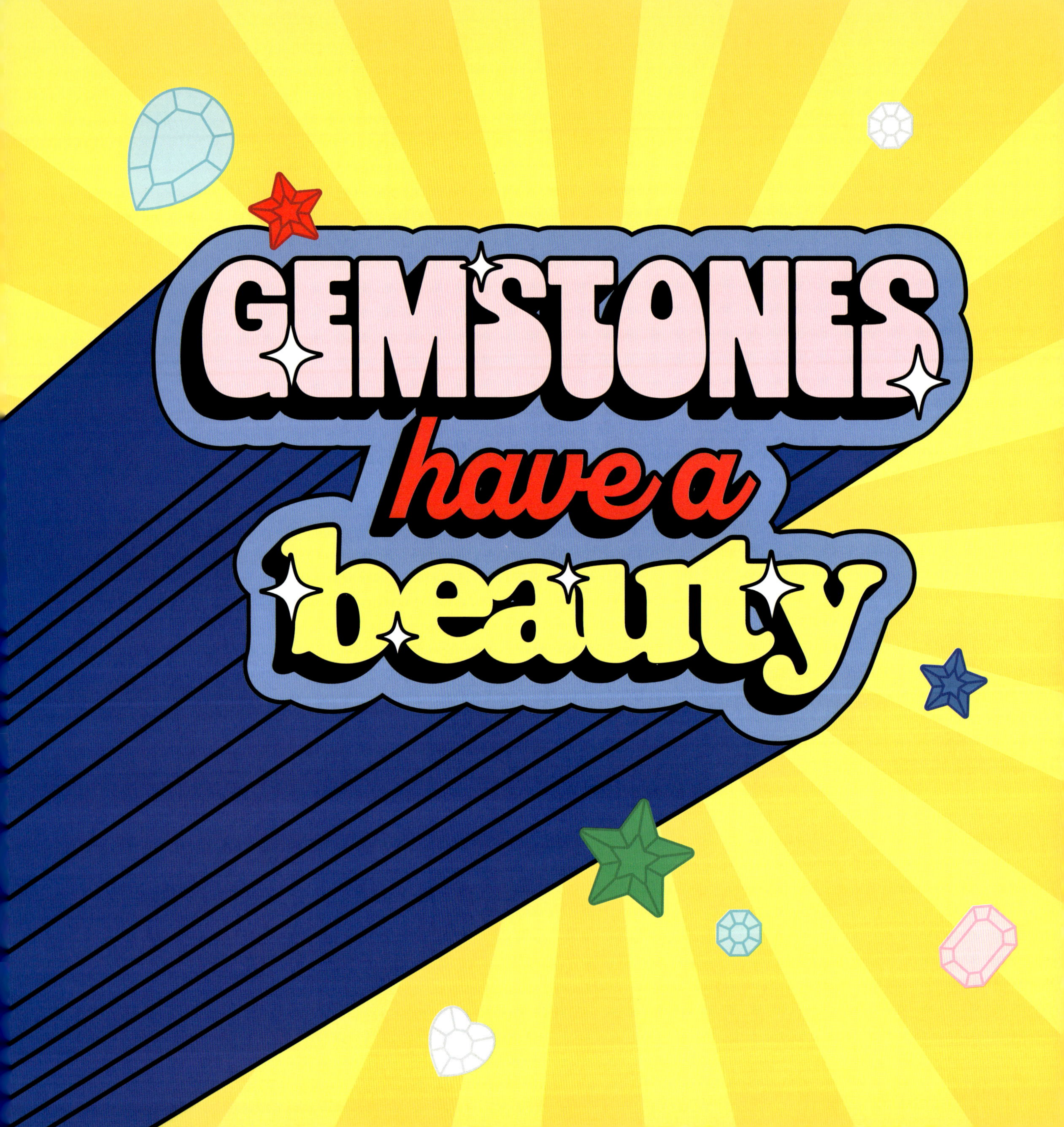
GEMSTONES
have a
beauty

that is
second
only to the
STARS

# December Turquoise

**December** dazzlers, your birthstone, turquoise, is a magical charm that brings good luck and protects its wearer from harm. Turquoise symbolizes protection, friendship, and good luck, and has even been believed to be an effective healer. Turquoise occurs naturally in places where acidic water meets copper, forming veins or nuggets of stone. Even with a blue color as rich as a cloudless sky, turquoise gems feel grounded with an earthly power. This is a superhero gemstone for safety and health, with the added bonus of strengthening friendships.

*Irene Neuwirth hand-carved turquoise flower necklace*

**Lol!**

**Did you know that turquoise is the best color?**

It's been cyan-tifically proven.

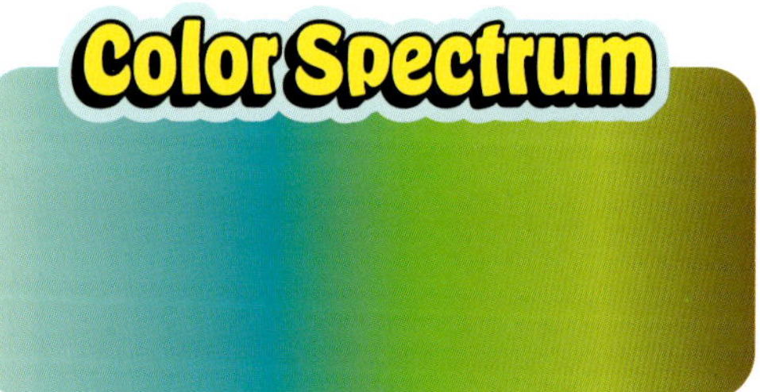

*Retrouvai turquoise "Talisman Clover" pendant*

*Jenna Blake three-stone emerald and turquoise ring*

## Fun Fact!

**Native American cultures have long valued turquoise, considering it a sacred stone with spiritual properties.**

## Color Spectrum

**Turquoise comes in a range of colors, from bright blue to green, with spots or veins created by different minerals like copper and iron.**

*Emily P. Wheeler turquoise and diamond bracelet*

Cartier turquoise and diamond ring

David Webb cabochon pink opal, turquoise, diamond, gold, and platinum earrings

Diné (Navajo) turquoise and silver bracelet

Irene Neuwirth triple-strand turquoise beaded "Candy" necklace

Diné (Navajo) turquoise and silver bracelet

Antique turquoise, diamond, sapphire, and ruby peacock brooch



## Symbolism & Meaning

**Protection, good fortune, communication, and success**

**Believed to promote mental and emotional clarity, enhance intuition, and provide spiritual grounding**

## Specs

| CHEMICAL COMPOSITION | HARDNESS |
| --- | --- |
| Hydrated copper aluminum phosphate | 5–6 on the Mohs' scale |

# Gem Atlas: A World Tour of Precious Stones

Welcome to Earth's Gemstone Gallery! This map showcases our planet's precious stones, each region a unique geological treasure chest.

Colombia's emeralds form when beryllium-rich rocks mix with chromium during tectonic collisions. Sri Lanka, the "Gem Island," is a sapphire and ruby hotspot. Australia's opals emerged from ancient seabeds, while South Africa's diamonds rocketed to the surface in fast-moving volcanic pipes. Myanmar's rubies formed in marble belts through intense metamorphism. Tanzania boasts tanzanite, found nowhere else on Earth!

Each dot on this map represents a gem location and a window into Earth's dynamic past, revealing the incredible processes that have shaped our world over eons.

### United States

- Diamond
- Garnet
- Opal
- Ruby
- Sapphire
- Agate
- Tourmaline
- Turquoise

### Colombia

- Emerald

### Brazil

- Tourmaline
- Opal
- Emerald
- Agate
- Amethyst
- Citrine

## STONE STRONGHOLDS: The World's Gemstone Hotspots

**90%** of aquamarines are produced in Brazil.

**95%** of opals are produced in Australia.

Over **90%** of the world's rubies come from Myanmar, making it the ruby capital of the world.

Colombia produces more than **70%** of the world's emeralds, despite its mines covering less than **1%** of the country.

Fun Fact!
Diamonds can be found on almost every continent, from the icy landscapes of Canada to the scorching heat of Africa and Australia.
Russia
Diamond
Emerald
Alexandrite
Ethiopia
Opal
Emerald
Sapphire
Garnet
Tourmaline
Pakistan
Emerald
Ruby
India
Diamond
Sapphire
Ruby
Emerald
NIGERIA
Tourmaline
Sapphire
Aquamarine
Emerald
Ruby
Sri Lanka
Sapphire
Ruby
MYANMAR
Jade
Ruby
Sapphire
ZAMBIA
Emerald
Kenya
Amethyst
Ruby
Aquamarine
Sapphire
Garnet
Tourmaline
TANZANIA
Tanzanite
Ruby
Sapphire
MOZAMBIQUE
Ruby
Madagascar
Sapphire
Ruby
Australia
Opal
Sapphire

# December
# Tanzanite

December discoverers, your birthstone is the mesmerizing tanzanite. A gem that sparkles with the vibrant violet and blue hues of a late-summer sunset and carries the magic of transformation—that's tanzanite. Throughout history, tanzanite has been thought to inspire a sense of exploration and bring a touch of spirituality to those who wear it. Tanzanite is a gem of self-discovery—encouraging its wearer to look within, fostering insight, and opening up new perspectives. This is the gemstone to seek out for a burst of inspiration.

*FoundRae yellow gold and tanzanite heart pendant*

*Tiffany & Co. tanzanite and diamond ring*

**Haha!**

**What did the tanzanite wear to sleep?**

A tanzanite-gown.

## Fun Fact!

**Tanzanite was discovered relatively recently, in 1967, making it one of the newest members of the birthstone family.**

*Unsigned antique tanzanite and diamond swan brooch*

## Color Spectrum

**This gemstone is pleochroic, meaning it can show different colors (reddish brown, blue, and violet) when viewed from different angles.**

*Verdura gold, tanzanite, and garnet three-stone ring*

*Buccellati tanzanite and diamond earrings set in yellow and white gold*

## Fun Fact!

**Oh, no! Geologists estimate that Earth's known tanzanite deposits may be depleted within the next few decades.**

## Symbolism & Meaning

**Transformation, spirituality, and exploration**

**Believed to stimulate insight and open up new perspectives**

*FoundRae tanzanite necklace*

*Tiffany & Co. tanzanite and diamond necklace*

*Eva Fehren tanzanite, blackened platinum, and white diamond pavé "Indigo Eclat" ring*

## Specs

| CHEMICAL COMPOSITION | HARDNESS |
| --- | --- |
| Calcium aluminum silicate | 6.5–7 on the Mohs' scale |

The
WORLD
is FULL
of MAGIC
THINGS,

patiently waiting for our senses to

GROW SHARPER

— W. B. YEATS

## ACKNOWLEDGMENTS

As sisters, we share a special shorthand—a language built on memories and connections that only we understand. We are deeply grateful to have been placed on this earth alongside each other, to create magic as a team. Thank you to all the forces that have guided us here—both seen and unseen.

We set out to capture the wonder we felt for these natural treasures and to celebrate the artists who carry on that beauty through new creations, too.

To our families—you've been our foundation. You've read drafts, offered feedback, brought endless tea and steadfast reassurance.

Gabi, Rafa, Luna, Silvi, and Isa—your infectious curiosity and energy have been the spark behind so much of what we create. This book exists because you exist.

Antonio, Papá, your encouragement to dream big and embrace hard work has always inspired us to reach higher. Rosaria, Mamá, your boundless creativity and optimism have been a constant source of peace and buoyancy in our lives. Diego, you led the way for us on creativity, modeling the virtues of making things—with your voice, with your hands, with your mind. It's never just the two of us; you are each always embedded in the work we do.

Noam and Jordan—you've been our unwavering partners. You've stood beside us through every wild idea and challenge. You are the invisible scaffolding that holds up all our efforts. You celebrate every win, cushion every loss, and remind us always of what really matters.

To our team at Super Smalls—"thank you" will never suffice. Together, we are motivated to make magic. To those who worked tirelessly on this: Kristin, Parisa, Madeline, Danielle, Lara—it's loaded with sparkle thanks to you. A special heartfelt thank-you to Kristin and Parisa: You're at the center of this work—your creative genius, dedication, and skill have elevated our pages.

Stellene, having you write our foreword is an honor. Olly and Sotheby's, thank you for believing and becoming the springboard for our vision. To the jewelers whose work is featured—your artistry has added brilliance that words alone could never achieve.

To our publishing team, thank you for your expertise and encouragement.

To our readers—this book is for you. We hope it inspires you to ask questions, explore deeply, share your discoveries, and find wonder in the everyday.

## IMAGE CREDITS

AKG-images: van Ham/Saša Fuis, Köln: 92 bottom right (opal leaf pin), 115 (turquoise peacock brooch)

Alamy: IanDagnall Computing: 109 (Cullinan diamond); The Print Collector: 109 (Royal Sceptre)

Courtesy of American Museum of Natural History: 59 center (pearl corsage brooch), 96 (orange fire opal, purple boulder opal, blue boulder opal, raw fire opal)

AP Images: Vincent Yu: 78 (Pink Star)

Art Resource: © RMN-Grand Palais: 50 bottom right (Bapst emerald tiara); V & A Images, London: 64 bottom (Man in the Moon brooch)

Courtesy of Jenna Blake: 114 right middle (turquoise and emerald ring)

Courtesy of Sophie Bille Brahe: 59 top right ("Botticelli" pearl earrings)

Bridgeman Images: Christie's Images/Private Collection: 38 bottom right (diamond frog brooch), 105 top right (citrine necklace), 108 (closed Fabergé egg); Kremlin Museums, Russia: 108 (open Fabergé egg); Lebrecht History: 109 (Royal Crown); Smithsonian Institution, Washington, DC, USA (Hope diamond)

Courtesy of Buccellati: 32 bottom left (aquamarine ring), © Aplomb Photo Studio: 25 middle center (amethyst bracelet), 77 top left (peridot pendant necklace), 93 top left (opal pendant necklace), 105 top left (citrine bracelet), 119 top left (tanzanite earrings)

Courtesy of Bulgari: 33 top right (aquamarine necklace), 98 bottom right (pink tourmaline ring), 99 center (pink tourmaline necklace)

Courtesy of Cleveland Museum of Art: Gift of the Hiller-Borneman Collection: 25 middle left (House of Fabergé amethyst pendant)

Courtesy of Crystal Caves: 79 (Empress of Uruguay)

DigitalVison Vectors: Medina Creatives (map)

E+: benedek: 35 (tiger's eye rectangle); ivstiv: 23 (amethyst polished); SunChan: 4, 27, back cover (pink tourmaline cushion), 5, 30, 34 (aquamarine oval), 8, 101 (topaz pear), 14, 23 (amethyst pear), 22 (amethyst oval), 34, 101 (amethyst rectangle), 48 (emerald round, emerald oval), 101 (emerald rectangle), 111 (tanzanite ovals)

Courtesy of Eva Fehren: 119 bottom left (tanzanite ring)

Courtesy of FoundRae: 77 top right (peridot pear medallion), 118 bottom left (tanzanite heart pendant), 119 top right (tanzanite necklace)

Courtesy of Gemfields: 14 (ruby oval), 48 (emerald pear, emerald chunk, emerald raw), 49 (emerald square), 66 (ruby ovals), 67 (ruby raw, ruby chunk, ruby ovals), 116 (emerald raw)

Gemological Institute of America: 35 (jade slab, rose quartz oval), 46 (spectrum chart, gray blue diamond tapered oval, blue violet diamond heart, pink purple diamond oval, purple diamond rectangle, red purple diamond round, violet diamond free-form, gray diamond oval, green blue diamond cushion, green blue diamond pear, blue green diamond cushion, blue diamond rectangle), 47 ( blue green diamond rectangle, yellow green diamond pear, greenish blue diamond princess, yellow green diamond cushion, yellow diamond cushion, orange diamond pear, yellow orange diamond pear, orange yellow diamond cushion, yellow orange oval diamond, purple pink diamond pear, red orange diamond round, purple red diamond Asscher, red diamond cushion), 62 (spiny oyster pearls), 63 (South Sea shell and pearl, Tahitian pearl and shell, Akoya shell and pearl), 86 (sapphire cushion, sapphire oval, green sapphire cushion, yellow sapphire cushion, golden sapphire cushion, yellow sapphire rectangle), 87 (orange sapphire square, pink purple sapphire square, magenta sapphire oval, light purple sapphire oval, purple sapphire cushion), 97 (blue and orange multicolor opal oval)

Getty Images: Graphic Artis: 109 (Koh i Noor); ISHARA S. KODIKARA: 78 (Star of Adam); GUILLERMO LEGARIA: 79 (Fura emerald); Eric-Paul-Pierre PASQUIER: 78 (Golden Jubilee); Alex Wong: 108 (Dresden diamond);

iStock/Getty Images Plus: 1000ways: 34 (gold labradorite); Aeya: 4 (diamond heart); Aksidesign: 27 (citron trilliant, tanzanite trilliant); alexhstock: 73 (turquoise); Aratehortua: 54, 55 (zodiac); ArgenLant: 72 (jasper), 102 (golden citrine raw); ARTKucherenko: 56 (white baroque pearl); avagyanlevon: 27 (red diamond Asscher, aquamarine Asscher); Peddalanka Ramesh Babu: 46 (black diamond); barbaraaaa: 30 (aquamarine chunks), 31 (aquamarine rectangle), 90 (pink tourmaline slice), 91 (pink tourmaline oval), 101 (emerald rock), 103 (citrine geode, citrine oval); Mehmet Gökhan Bayhan: 110 (turquoise rock), 111 (turquoise rock); Byjeng: 4, 26 (topaz marquise), 9 (blue sapphire pear, violet sapphire oval), 9, 10 (purple sapphire oval), 10, 26 (aquamarine pear), 11 (citrine rectangle), 16 (garnet rectangle), 22, 25 bottom right (amethyst oval), 26 (diamond round), 26 (peridot princess, sapphire pear, ruby pear), 27 (citrine heart), 27, back cover (emerald heart), 27 (sapphire oval, ruby oval, sapphire cushion), 27, 49 (emerald rectangle), 66 (ruby round, ruby side), 66, 67 (ruby pear), 82 (sapphire cushion), 83 (sapphire pear), 87 (orange red sapphire oval), 101 (sapphire oval), back cover (garnet, sapphire, topaz), 86 (sapphire oval, sapphire square cushion, sapphire rectangle cushion, sapphire pear, sapphire round), 101 (citrine gem); Liudmila Chernetska: 57 (pearl in shell); Creativeye99: 62 (quahog clamshell); Thomas Demarczyk: 96, 100 (white raw opal); DiamondGalaxy: 8, 9, 10, 11, 39 (diamond round), 16 (garnet round), 25 (amethyst round), 54, 55, 116, 117 (round gems), 33 (aquamarine round), 42 (diamond profile), 43 (blue diamond), 47 (pink diamond side), 51 (emerald round), 69 (ruby round), 77 (peridot round), 85 (sapphire round), 99 (pink tourmaline round), 105 (citrine round), 119 (tanzanite round); DNY59: 91 (pink tourmaline square); fenkep: 5, 15, 110 (tanzanite trilliant); habrda: 100 (dark pearl); hapalena: 102, 103 (citrine raw); Igor_Kali: 14 (peridot trilliant), 74 (peridot round side, peridot heart, peridot square), 102 (citrine round tilted, citrine round), 103 (citrine round side); Ikonacolor: 9, 14, 26, 31 (aquamarine marquise), 102 (citrine round side); ivstiv: 73 (amber); J-Palys: 22, 23 (amethyst chunk), 35 (rose quartz crystal); Mark S Johnson: 46 (black diamond marquise); jopelka (rose quartz raw); Kerrick: 16, 35 (garnet raw), 72, 73 (rhodochrosite); Knaupe: 72 (tiger's eye); Çağla Köshserli: 72 (malachite); KrimKate: 34 (onyx polished), 34, 91, 97 (opal slab), 35 (peridot polished), 55, 116 (turquoise round), 72 (lapis lazuli polished), 75 (peridot raw), 82 (sapphire raw), 110 (tanzanite, turquoise rectangle), 111 (tanzanite raw, turquoise polished), 115 (turquoise round); Marina Krisenko: 63 (freshwater shell); Laures: 34 (amethyst polished); lermannika: 27 (pink tourmaline oval), 34 (lapis lazuli triangle); Sergey Lifanov: 26 (diamond princess), 27 (diamond rectangle); magnetcreative: 62 (conch shell); MarcelC: 34 (lapis lazuli polished), 90, 97 (blue green opal); Martinan: 35, 101 (rose quartz polished); Dmitrii Maslov: 34 (onyx round); mikheewnik: 10 (mauve sapphire cushion), 83 (sapphire cushion), 86 (sapphire rectangle, sapphire cushion), 87 (yellow orange sapphire oval, pink sapphire oval, violet sapphire cushion); mindelio: 16 (garnet pear, upside-down gem), 11, 15, 26 (pink tourmaline princess); Model-la: 11 (diamond square), 36 (diamond cushion, diamond baguette, diamond Asscher, diamond rectangle), 36, 37 (diamond round, diamond marquise), 37 (diamond rectangle, diamond heart)); nastya: 35 (tiger's eye polished); olivermohr: 34 (labradorite oval, lapis lazuli round); oxign: 91 (oval opal); PeterHermesFurian: 34 (amethyst raw); RatreeFuang: 35 (jade polished); real444: 27 (pink tourmaline heart); retouchman: 36 (diamond raw), 101 (diamond raw, diamond pear); Rozaliya: 47 (cognac diamond point); Minakryn Ruslan: 8, 14 (garnet cushion), 17, 35 (garnet cushion), 31, 34 (aquamarine oval); sharpness71: 34, 90, 96 (multicolor triangular opal), 97 (multicolor triangular opal); Dmitrii Stoliarevich: 27 (yellow diamond Asscher); sundrawlex: 35, 100 (striped amber); Liza Tkachuk: 27 (emerald trilliant); TomekD76: 97, 116 (multicolor opal chunk); ToscaWhi: 8, 9, 10, 11, 15, 55 (pearl), 57 (white and pink pearls); Anna Usova: 102 (yellow citrine raw); VvoeVale: 31, 35 (aquamarine polished), 35 (jade rectangle, peridot rock), 73 (orbicular agate); Warren_Price: 62 (spiny oyster shell); WojciechMY: 72, 116 (Apache agate); Bjoern Wylezich: 34 (aquamarine raw); xelf: 17 (garnet round); xtrekx: 101 (ruby round side); Thomas Yeoh: 43 (diamond border); YolandaVanNiekerk: 23 (amethyst oval); yrabota: 35 (yellow amber, golden amber)

Courtesy of Harwell Godfrey: 92 top (opal necklace)

Courtesy of Oscar Heyman: 32 top left (aquamarine ring), 93 middle right (opal swan brooch)

Courtesy of Monica Rich Kosann: 92 bottom left (opal frog ring)

Courtesy of Marlo Laz: 18 left (garnet necklace), 39 (diamond and gold ring), 77 center (peridot starburst necklace), 85 left (sapphire necklace), 99 top left (pink tourmaline earrings)

Courtesy of Elizabeth Locke: 77 top center (peridot ring), 98 bottom left (pink tourmaline ring)

Courtesy of Material Good: 104 top left (citrine earrings)

Courtesy of Mikimoto: 33 top left (aquamarine ring), 39 bottom left (diamond ring), 58, 59 (pearl and diamond collar), 59 left (classic pearl necklace), 62 top right (conch pearl), 62 (orange melo melo pearl)

Courtesy of Minneapolis Institute of Art: 115 bottom left (turquoise Navajo bracelets)

Courtesy of Brent Neale: 64 top (moonstone mushroom and heart pendants), 105 top middle (citrine ring)

Courtesy of Irene Neuwirth: 65 center right (moonstone bracelet), 77 bottom left (peridot ring), 85 top right (sapphire earrings), 104 bottom left (citrine necklace), 114 (turquoise flower necklace), 115 (turquoise necklace)

Courtesy of Perlas del Mar de Cortez: 63 (Sea of Cortez shell and pearls)

Courtesy of Briony Raymond: 39 top right (diamond ring), 85 top middle (sapphire ring)

Courtesy of Retrouvai: 51 top right (emerald earrings), 68 bottom (ruby bracelet); 114 left (turquoise clover pendant)

Courtesy of Reza: 51 center (emerald ring), 69 middle right (ruby ring), 85 center middle (sapphire earrings)

Shutterstock: Levon Avagyan: cover, 3, 15 (emerald rectangle), 14, 82 (sapphire Asscher), 46 (green blue rectangle), 82 (sapphire round side); Balonici: 47 (orange round diamond); boykung: 47 (champagne diamond cushion, champagne diamond round); Manutsawee Buapet: cover, 3, 5, 8, back cover (diamond round); Byjeng: cover, 3, 83, 85 bottom right (sapphire oval), 2, 30, 33 bottom right (aquamarine round), 2, 37, 39 bottom right (diamond Asscher), 2 (pink tourmaline round, garnet oval, sapphire pear), 2, 49, 51 bottom right (emerald heart), 3 (amethyst oval), 3, 37, 39 bottom right (diamond heart), 3, 31, 33 (aquamarine cushion), 5, 15 (citrine rectangle), 8, 9, 11 (diamond asscher), 9, 10 (magenta sapphire cushion), 15 (diamond heart), 17, 19 bottom right (garnet trapezoid), 91, 99 bottom right (pink tourmaline round side), 119 bottom right (tanzanite pear); Somjit Chomram: 35 (jade oval); Chursina Viktoriia: 57 (baroque pearl); Stewart Cook: 50, 51 (Bulgari emerald necklace and pendant); Darkydoors: 96 (yellow opal oval, blue opal oval, multicolor opal triangle, multicolor opal oval), 97 (light blue multicolor opal oval, blue polished opal); J.T. Davis: 35 (tiger's eye slab); DmitrySt: 37, 39 (diamond raw), 46 (diamond marquise), 47 (pink diamond side, pink diamond oval, diamond marquise); Fruit Cocktail Creative: 63 (black South Sea pearl); galka3250: 86 (green sapphire pear), 87 (light purple sapphire oval, violet sapphire triangle, violet sapphire pear, light violet sapphire oval, dark violet sapphire triangle, violet sapphire heart), 103 (yellow citrine oval); GRAPHICS COLLECTION: 118 bottom right (tanzanite swan brooch); Imfoto: 16 (garnet chunk); Jota_Visual: 73 (watermelon tourmaline); Joyisjoyful: 110 (tanzanite pear); Henri Koskinenen: 16, 17 (garnets raw); KrimKate: 56 (moonstone raw); luca85: 17 (garnet geode); Abdul Matloob: 54, 93, 116, 117 (opal round); NickKnight: cover, back cover (blue zircon round), cover, 3, 91, 99 bottom right: (pink tourmaline marquise), cover, 2, 8, (topaz heart), 27, 83 (sapphire heart), 82 (sapphire oval), 83 (sapphire round), 86 (olive green sapphire rectangle); OMG_Studio: 9, 10, 86 (green sapphire oval); optimarc: 115 bottom right (turquoise polished); photo-world: 66, 69 bottom right, 116 (ruby raw), 83, 85 bottom right (sapphire raw); photo33mm: 9, 10, 11 (white sapphire oval), 10 (sapphire oval), 11, 86 (light green sapphire oval), 11, 97 (magenta sapphire rectangle), 86 (sapphire oval, sapphire rectangle, sapphire oval, green sapphire rectangle, orange sapphire oval), 87 (pink sapphire oval); Minakryn Ruslan: 17 (garnet raw); Atiketta Sangasaeng: 26 (ruby marquise); Azlan Shehzad: 46 (blue rectangle, yellow rectangle); STUDIO492: cover, 4, 26, back cover (amethyst round), cover, 2, 3, 5, 55, 56, 59 bottom right, 100, back cover (pearl), cover, 5, 11, 66, 69 (ruby round), 4 (peridot oval), 11, 91, 100 (opal oval), 11, 103, 105 bottom right (citrine oval), 19, 35 (garnet round), 27 (emerald cushion);

Van Rossen: 63 (Tahitian pearls); vvoe: 15 (moonstone oval), 15, 84 (turquoise oval), 55, 57, 65 bottom right (moonstone round), 56 (moonstone slab), 100 (turquoise raw, turquoise polished); Edward Westmacott: cover, 2, 47 (pink diamond round)

Courtesy of the Smithsonian Institute/National Museum of Natural History: 11, 15 (white opal oval), 74 (peridot pear, peridot rectangle), 96 (free-form white opal, pink opal), 97 (pink opal, blue opal, orange opal oval); Chip Clark: 73 (Apache agate), 97 (opal fossil, opal in rock, green Roebling opal); Ken Larsen: 8, 35, 75 (peridot tapered rectangle), 30 (aquamarine cushion), 62 bottom left (conch pearl), 75 (peridot oval), 97 (abstract white opal)

Courtesy of Sotheby's: 18, 19 (Asprey garnet necklace), 19 (Bulgari garnet earrings, Tiffany & Co. garnet ring, Pomellato garnet ring), 24 top (Tiffany & Co. amethyst ring), 24 bottom right (Cartier amethyst turtle brooch), 24 bottom middle (Chanel amethyst ring), 24 left (Van Cleef & Arpels amethyst bracelet), 25 top right (Bulgari amethyst earrings), 25 left (Cartier amethyst necklace), 32, 33 (Van Cleef & Arpels aquamarine necklace), 32 (Verdura aquamarine heart brooch); 33 center (Van Cleef & Arpels aquamarine earrings and brooch), 38 center (Bulgari diamond snake necklace), 39 top (Van Cleef & Arpels zipper necklace), 50 center (Bulgari emerald ring), 51 top left (Van Cleef & Arpels emerald bird brooches), 58 bottom right (Seaman Schepps pearl bird brooch), 58 bottom left (Harry Winston pearl earrings), 65 middle left (Jewels by JAR moonstone earrings), 65 top left (Verdura moonstone ring), 68 top (Van Cleef & Arpels ruby flower brooch), 69 left (Van Cleef & Arpels ruby and diamond necklace), 69 center left (Graff ruby earrings), 76 bottom right (Cartier peridot panther ring), 84 center (Cartier sapphire leopard ring), 84 bottom (Tiffany & Co. sapphire butterfly brooches), 98 center (Verdura pink tourmaline heart), 99 top right (Seaman Schepps pink tourmaline necklace), 104 top (Jewels by JAR citrine necklace), 104 bottom right (Tiffany & Co. citrine Bird on a Rock), 105 bottom left (Marina B citrine collar), 115 top left (Cartier turquoise ring), 118, 119 (Tiffany & Co. tanzanite necklace), 118 top right (Tiffany & Co. tanzanite ring), 118 bottom left (Verdura tanzanite ring)

Courtesy of Glenn Spiro: 19 bottom left (garnet bracelet), 39 left (diamond earrings), 69 top right (ruby bracelet), 69 bottom center (ruby ring), 84 top (sapphire necklace)

Courtesy of Sylva & Cie: 64 bottom, 65 (moonstone bracelet), 93 top right (opal necklace)

Courtesy of the Walters Art Museum: 18 top (garnet intaglio ring)

Courtesy of David Webb: 76 top (peridot cuff), 93 bottom left (opal cuff), 115 middle right (turquoise earrings)

Courtesy of Emily P. Wheeler: 18 bottom (garnet cuff), 38 top (pink necklace with diamonds), 65 top right (moonstone chubby ring), 76 bottom left (peridot earrings), 114 (turquoise bracelet)

Courtesy of Wikimedia Commons: 108 (Daria-e-Noor); Azuncha: 74, 77 bottom right (peridot raw); Mauro Cateb: 25 bottom right (amethyst square); Stephanie Clifford: 30, 33 bottom right, 116 (aquamarine raw); Gems21: 48, 51 bottom right (emerald rectangle); Global Gemology: 62 top left (conch pearl), 62 (quahog pearls); H.Zell: 62 (melo melo shell); Human feather: 75, 77 bottom right (peridot rectangle); Jennifergaglione: 63 (freshwater pearls); JJ Harrison: 22, 25 bottom right (amethyst raw); Sasaki kijinuko: 67, 69 bottom right (ruby oval); Robert M. Lavinsky: 19 bottom right (garnet raw), 51 bottom right (emerald raw), 57, 65 (moonstone raw), 90, 99 bottom right (pink tourmaline raw), 101 (topaz raw), 115 bottom right (turquoise slab), 119 bottom right (tanzanite raw); Liné1: 62 (melo melo pearls); Pawel Maliszczak: 102, 103, 105 bottom right (golden citrine chunk); James St. John: 74, 77 bottom right (peridot rock), 90, 93 bottom right (opal raw)

Courtesy of Jemma Wynne: 38 bottom left (diamond and gold wave ring), 99 center left (pink tourmaline necklace)

# REFERENCES


## BOOKS

Bonewitz, R. *The Rock and Gem Book: Treasures of the Natural World*. DK, 2016.

Crowe, Judith. *The Jeweller's Directory of Gemstones.* *Herbert Press, Quarto Publishing plc*, London, 2006.

*Crystal and Gem (DK Eyewitness)*. DK Children, 2023

*Crystal Magic: Discover the Secret World of Crystals.* Welbeck Children's Books, UK, 2024.

*Emerald*. Thames & Hudson, 2014, reprinted 2016.

Hall, Judith. *The Encyclopedia of Crystals*. Hachette UK, 2013.

———. *The Little Book of Crystals*. Hachette UK, 2016.

Hansen, Robin. *The Natural History Museum Book of Gemstones: A Concise Reference Guide*. Natural History Museum, London, 2022, reprinted 2023.

Hardy, J., and J. Self. *Emerald: Twenty-One Centuries of Jeweled Opulence and Power*. Thames & Hudson, 2013.

Hardy, Joanna, and Robert Violette. *Sapphire: A Celebration of Colour*. Thames & Hudson, 2021.

Hardy, Joanna. *Ruby: The King of Gems*. Thames & Hudson, 2017, reprinted 2021, 2022.

*Jewel: The Definitive Visual Guide*. DK London, Penguin Random House, 2023.

*Rocks and Minerals: The Essential Facts and Stats on More Than 200 of Earth's Natural Treasures*. DK London, Penguin Random House, 2023.

Smithsonian. *Minerals, Gemstones and Jewels*. Penguin Random House, 2018.

*The Rock and Gem Box: 10 Books Set*. DK Children's, London, n.d.

Vollandes, Stellene. *Jewels That Made History*. Rizzoli, 2020.

## WEBSITES AND BLOGS

American Gem Society, americangemsociety.org.

American Museum of Natural History, amnh.org.

Gem Rock Auctions, gemrockauctions.com.

Gemological Institute of America (GIA), gia.edu.

Geological Society of America, geosociety.org.

International Gem Society, gemsociety.org.

John Betts Fine Minerals, johnbetts-fineminerals.com.

Mark Schneider Design, markschneiderdesign.com.

Smithsonian Institution, si.edu.

Smithsonian Magazine. smithsonianmag.com.

Stone Mania UK, stonemania.co.uk.

Wikipedia, wikipedia.org.

ISBN 978-1-4549-5798-0

Library of Congress Cataloging-in-Publication Data is available



Printed in China

10 9 8 7 6 5 4 3 2 1

unionsquareandco.com
supersmalls.com

Design by Parisa Dale and Stacy Forte